DAVID LEADBETTER

100%
Golf

DAVID LEADBETTER

100%
Golf

· UNLOCKING YOUR TRUE GOLF POTENTIAL ·

David Leadbetter

with Richard Simmons

Photography by David Cannon

Foreword by Ernie Els

HarperResource
An Imprint of HarperCollins*Publishers*

100% GOLF:
UNLOCKING YOUR TRUE GOLF POTENTIAL

FIRST EDITION

Library of Congress Cataloguing-In-Publication
has been applied for.

ISBN 0-06-270823-6 646-9

02 03 04 05 06 10 9 8 7 6 5 4 3 2 1

Colour origination by Digital Imaging
Designed by Robert Kelland
Printed and bound in Italy by Rotolito Lombarda

• CONTENTS •

· FOREWORD ·

By Ernie Els

David Leadbetter needs no introduction. His unique ability to help golfers of all ages and abilities to play better golf and get more fun out of the game is legendary the world over. And let's not underestimate that 'fun' element; quite apart from helping his students to understand the reasoning behind certain aspects of swing technique, one of David's great qualities is that he never forgets this is a game. A tough game, sure. But a game we

love to play, and one that promises all of us a great deal of enjoyment and satisfaction.

My association with David goes back to the early 1990s when I called him up and asked if he would help me to iron out one or two problems I was struggling with. I don't consider myself to be a particularly technical thinker when it comes to maintaining my swing, and I was refreshed to discover that David's approach pretty much reflected my own. His clear-cut advice was as simple as it was logical. Nothing fancy, nothing so complicated it might blow my mind. Just down to earth common sense that gave me a fresh perspective on swinging the club and playing the game – right the way from tee to green.

And that is what this book can do for you. Whether you are fresh to the adventure or in search of a new direction, the lessons you are about to experience have been written in such a concise manner they can do nothing but help you to grasp and develop the basic skills of the game. For every golfer who ever picked up a club, these are the simple facts of life, if you like. Short of jumping on a plane and making the trip to David's Academy headquarters, at Champions' Gate in Florida, I'd say this is the second best thing to a one-on-one with the man many regard as the finest coach in the world today.

Myself included.

· INTRODUCTION ·

By David Leadbetter

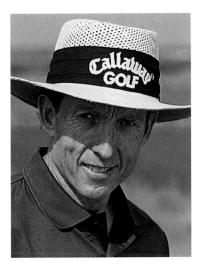

*I*s this game driving you crazy? Are you tired of making the same old mistakes every time you go out to play? Do you step up to the tee confused by too much technical information? Is a general lack of consistency through the bag the hallmark of your game? When invited to play business or corporate golf, is your overriding goal not to be too embarrassed? Do family and work commitments leave you with relatively little time to play and practice? Are you one of those players who has all the latest gear, but still have a hard time breaking 90? Is that short walk from the practice ground to the first tee nothing short of a journey into the unknown?

If the answer to any of the above is 'yes', then this book is for you. What you are about to experience is a crash course in all the skills that you need to get started, or to turn your game around, or even as a general refresher presented in a format that I hope players of all ages and ability will find both entertaining and easy to understand.

It's no secret that most of my teaching these days is spent working with tour players, talented amateurs and juniors, but, believe me, I also spend a good deal of time working with corporate groups and individuals just like yourself – weekend golfers who know it is within their power to play a better game, but who simply don't know how. Unlocking that potential is the ultimate test of our day-to-day business at the David Leadbetter Golf Academy sites around the world, and it's also the grounding essence of this book – *100% Golf*.

There's no getting away from the fact that you get a certain buzz working with the game's top players, and over the years I have been lucky enough to spend time with some of the very best – major champions Nick Faldo, Nick Price, Greg Norman, Ernie Els and Tom Watson among them. And I suppose it is because of this association at the highest level that I often find myself labelled as a technically-minded coach. I'm no stranger to swing theory, that's for sure – my first book, *The Golf Swing*, dealt more with the strict theory of the swing. As a matter of fact, in my early days as a professional, this preoccupation with mechanics was definitely a factor that hurt my own playing career; I was too much of a perfectionist, always tinkering, and keen to question how and why something worked (or didn't!), when I should have been focusing on making the best of what natural ability I had. But this inquisitive side to my character has been the making of my career as a teacher. As my own understanding has grown, so has my ability to simplify the details and to communicate what I believe are the essential 'musts' every golfer has to learn before he or she can fully appreciate the thrill of the game.

I don't suppose the notion that I am some sort of walking textbook is ever likely to go away. But if you

were to spend a little time watching me or one of my staff of instructors teach at my Academy headquarters at Champions' Gate, in Orlando, Florida, I think you might be surprised at just how non-technical our approach really is. Out on the range, my style is to paint in the mind of my students a series of images that help to clarify the movements and the sensations associated with making a solid, repeating swing.

Putting that across on paper has been the challenge in writing this, my sixth book, and my thanks go out to my co-writer Richard Simmons, and photographer David Cannon, for helping me to consolidate my thoughts so clearly and vividly. When it came to the initial editing stage, I was alarmed at how much

material hit the floor, but this wholesale decimation of information reflects what good teaching is all about – filtering out the jargon. As the final manuscript began to take shape, I found myself proof-reading exactly what I had hoped for: a concise, down to earth guide that won't tie you up in knots. *100% Golf* really is a book for the masses.

As you are about to discover, this is not a book that concerns itself too much in the way of theory, although there are occasions when you do need to at least understand the nuts-and-bolts reasoning behind what you are trying to achieve. Above all, it's a book full of simple thoughts and bold images that invites you to dip in and out of the various chapters as you wish, and as such it is perfect for those of you who have no desire to slave away on the practice tee, but who could use some help to get your game into a forward gear. Give these lessons a chance to sink in, and they will enable you to eliminate careless faults and replace them with good habits that improve your ball-striking, your short-game skills and your thinking on the course. The bottom line is that you will shoot lower scores, and that makes the game a lot more fun.

Where to begin? Well, that's easy. If we were meeting face to face, the first thing that would interest me is the quality of your grip and your general approach to setting up to the ball – golf's so-called fundamentals. So, following a 'blueprint' sequence designed to get the creative juices flowing, that's where we'll start. Moving on from these lessons, what little theory you do need to be aware of appears in Chapter 2, where I am going to show you how to go about piecing together a solid swing in a series of easy 'links' and checkpoints. Synchronizing the movement of the arms and the body is the key, and to get the most out of this section, I'd suggest that you keep a club handy so that you can copy me and get a feel for each of these positions as we work through them.

More emphasis in the beginning should be placed on the proper form and technique, and to this end I suggest that the ball should be taken out of the equation. The natural tendency is to want to hit a good solid shot, obviously, but this is often undertaken at the expense of proper technique, and the very presence of a ball can hinder the learning process. So, work on these moves at home in front of a full-length mirror. If you can spend five minutes three or four

times a week rehearsing these individual moves (or 'links', as I call them), I think you'll be amazed at just how quickly you have the makings of a good swing. After that, repetition is the only way to get better, and as so-called 'muscle memory' takes hold, it's then a matter of blending these moves together to create a continuous, flowing motion from start to finish. A good swing demands rhythm, basically, and to help you find it, I have included a number of drills that will help you and the golf club to move more freely and easily. Inventing these drills has become something of a trademark for me, and you will find quite a number of them scattered in the various chapters throughout the book. Each one is designed to help you attach good feelings to the correct motion without having to think too hard about the mechanics involved. They make practising more fun, and more meaningful, and utilizing them will help you to learn and understand more quickly.

More than anything, golf is a game of feelings and sensations. And it's a game that will test every ounce of your resolve and your patience, because what feels good one day has a habit of suddenly feeling awkward the next. There isn't a golfer alive who hasn't experienced the frustration that this game seems uniquely capable of dishing out, which is why good teaching deals mostly in simplicity. I sincerely hope that message comes across in this book. What's more, I believe that anyone who can grasp these lessons can improve his or her game with the minimal amount of practice – and if your lifestyle is anything like as hectic as mine, that must surely qualify as the ultimate 'win-win' deal.

David Leadbetter

My blueprint for a modern swing

**HOW TO IDENTIFY WITH THE QUALITIES
OF A NATURAL SWINGING MOTION THAT CAN BE APPLIED
TO EVERY CLUB IN THE BAG**

As a coach, everything that I tell my pupils is geared towards helping them to get the clubhead moving and swinging freely. To create a *flowing* motion. This might seem a rather obvious statement to make at the head of a book such as this, but let me back it up by saying that by far the greatest problem for most golfers (even some of the better ones) is that their chief swing thought is to kill the ball; they want to physically over-control the club and hit 'at' it, instead of trusting the forces at work in the swing, and letting the ball get in the way.

This distinction between 'swinging' and 'hitting' is an important one to make, and before we go on to look at the grip and the set-up, just stop for a minute and think about what you are actually trying to achieve here. The key word is *SWING* – which I like to describe as a synchronized movement of the club, the hands, the arms and the body that results in speed and momentum being released in the direction of the target. Every golfer learns this lesson sooner or later, but you will save yourself a lot of time and frustration if you take it on board before we go any further. You don't often hit good golf shots by aggressively hitting *at* the ball, more frequently, you hit good shots when you learn to swing the clubhead effortlessly through it.

Creating a free-flowing swing... naturally

How complicated a motion is it? Holding the club loosely between the thumb and the first two fingers on my right hand, and standing with my feet spread apart, knees slightly flexed and a gentle forward bend at the hips, all I am doing in the accompanying sequence is let the clubhead find its own way as I turn my upper body and swing my right arm up and down. Nothing could be easier: *'TURN AND SWING'*. I'm not thinking consciously about what I have to do to create this motion, it just happens.

Starting the clubhead a couple of feet forward helps me gather some early momentum, and the club works back smoothly on the inside track as it falls and continues to swing up on a good plane as the wrist hinges to arrive on line at the top of the backswing. Then, with a smooth, unhurried change of direction,

the clubhead naturally begins to accelerate as I reverse the momentum of the swing and release it all the way to a balanced finish.

I'm prepared to state up front that anyone capable of creating this simple motion is well on the way to making a decent golf swing. Go well down the grip of a short iron and try it: Hold the club loosely between the thumb and those two fingers, and really sense the weight of the head on the end of the shaft as you casually swing it back and forth. As the wrist hinges back on itself and the club swings up, you should be aware of it feeling almost weightless as it reaches this vertical position (here, it has found its natural 'balance point', a good sign that your swing is on track). Sense the shaft kiss the base of your neck as

you complete your backswing, and again as you unwind your body and release the right arm on the through-swing. Don't force the issue; simply let the clubhead swing and find its own way to the finish – the shape of the movement back and through should basically mirror one another.

The wonderful thing about this little exercise is that it encapsulates all of the good things you hope to achieve with both hands on the club, as long as you are prepared to let the swing unfold naturally. As I hinted a moment ago, the tendency (and the problem) for most golfers is to want to hold on too tight and over-control the motion. With just the thumb and those two fingers on the grip, that's simply not an option, and though we haven't even begun to talk in any

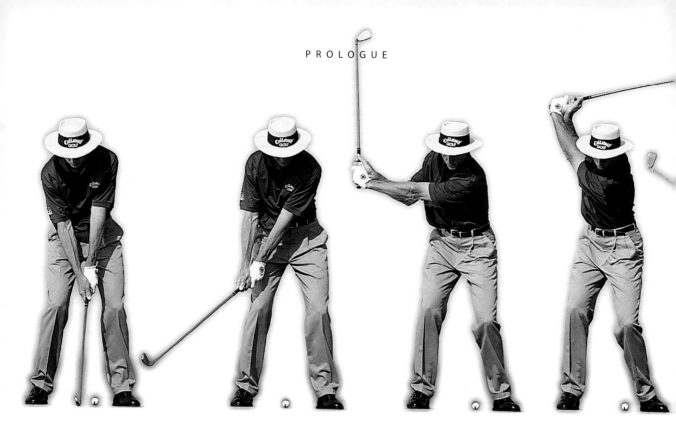

detail about how to make a swing, I hope this exercise at least gives you a sense of the basic shape and the freedom involved in swinging the club around your body with a good rhythm. All you have to do is find a grip that promotes the quality of this liaison between you and the club with *both* hands on board, along with the control and the stability of a well-ordered set-up position generally. Add in some body motion for power, and hey presto! You have a golf swing.

Freedom is motion – why rhythm is a golfer's best friend

Anyone who has ever played this game to a reasonable standard will tell you that the best golf always feels easy; that when they are striking the ball solidly, right out of the middle of the clubface, the entire motion feels effortless. The club feels light in the hands, and when a player is enjoying this sort of form, the mind is blissfully free of technical thoughts. I don't recall who is credited with this observation, but to me it sums it all up perfectly: *Good players swing easy, and hit hard*. And the easier they try to swing the club-

head, the better they seem to strike the ball. Contrast this with the experience of most weekend amateurs. When I look around, I see players who give the impression that they are trying to steer the club into certain positions, rather than swinging through them. They appear perpetually at odds with the club; there's no sense of rhythm or flow.

One of the reasons so many golfers fail to create a good basic motion is that they are victims of certain phrases that lead to damaging misconceptions about the swing. I'm talking about such popular clichés as *'Keep the left arm straight'*, and *'Keep your head still'*, *'Fold the right elbow'*, and so on. These are dangerous expressions, particularly when taken out of context. *'Make a big turn'* and *'Clear the hips for power'* are further examples that spring to mind. Although such thoughts may have some value attached to them, taking any of them too literally creates a mind-set that generally inhibits a player's ability to visualize the swing as one continuous free-flowing motion.

Whenever I am asked to define a golf swing I talk about it as being 'the synchronised turning of the body and swinging of the arms and hands'. Blending

these elements together in harmony is the ultimate challenge, and though no two swings are ever exactly alike, it is possible to identify a number of shared qualities in every dynamic action. A good swing 'flows' from the set-up position, and is geared towards maximizing clubhead speed where it matters most: at impact. I like to think of the rotary motion of the body as the engine that drives the swing, the arms and hands essentially free-wheeling in response, while a good wrist action conducts their speed to accelerate the clubhead squarely into the ball.

As you study the 'blueprint' sequences across these pages, pay particular attention to the way in which a good swing mixes geometry with art. The body angles that are established at the set-up are responsible for the general shape and consistency of your swing. Chief among these is the spine angle that is created as you bend from the hips at address, form-ing the axis about which the upper body rotates. That angle will naturally vary according to the length of the club you happen to be using, but the key at all times is to make the most of your height before bend-ing gently forwards and flexing your knees for

balance. As you stand to the ball, you want to feel that your arms hang with a certain 'softness', ready to *swing freely* as the body turns, while the width of the stance provides the necessary foundation for bal-ance. For practical purposes I like to regard the lower body as a suspension unit that stabilizes the swing – you want to feel 'springy' at address, the muscles in your thighs keyed-up and ready to offer support.

Looking face on, the arms clearly form the radius (or 'width') of the swing as the body turns back and then through to face the target. The clubhead traces a wide circular motion (maintaining that width is one of the keys to solid ball-striking) while the wrists provide the hinge that enables the club to swing up and down on a consistent plane. Turning the upper body over, the stability (and 'resistance') of the hips and knees creates what we describe as a 'coiling' effect. In the course of the backswing, the body effectively winds itself up like a spring. Then, through a subtle and unhurried change of direction, the gears are reversed, and there's a sense of 'elasticity' about the body as the changeover takes place and the spring is released. The dynamics of the recoil are such that the

Keynote qualities of a flowing swing

● **Ready to play**
The set-up position sees you and the club united in a state of athletic balance

● **Starting off**
To initiate momentum, the hands, arms and club move away *together*

● **Halfway house**
Relaxed hands and forearms allow the wrists to hinge, and the club swings up on a good plane

● **Solid at the top**
A full turn of the upper body creates 'coil', and completes the backswing motion

clubhead is then accelerated at terrific speed through the ball, the sheer momentum of the swing carrying you all the way to a full and rounded finish – again engineered in perfect balance.

Though still images will never truly capture the athleticism of a flowing motion, I hope these sequences will at least go some way towards galvanizing the notion that a good swing is in essence a 'chain reaction' in which one good move can be seen to lead to the next. As your only point of contact with the club, the grip is at the heart of the action. Clearly,

in order to swing that weight on the end of the shaft, you first have to be able to feel it.

Whether you are hitting a driver, a 6-iron or a wedge, the best advice is always to hold the club with a relatively light grip pressure that leaves the fingers sensitive to the weight of the clubhead. The hands, forearms and shoulders must be relaxed, ready to move and create a swing. That's the key word in all of this. The wrists are seen to hinge (or 'set' as I term it) in the backswing and that angle is retained until deep into the downswing when you no longer resist the

● Starting down
Always *flowing*, a good swing is seen to gather speed as the momentum is reversed

● Back to the ball
Angles originally created at the set-up are reflected at the moment of impact – at terrific speed

● The release
The club is now free-wheeling into the follow-through, the ball is on its way towards the target

● Follow through
Body continues to rotate all the way to the finish, a position of balance and control

centrifugal forces at work. This wrist cock multiplies the acceleration of the club on its way to impact – and maximizing that speed with a good wrist action is the secret to hitting long and solid shots with relatively little effort.

A sense of timing and coordination are the more artistic qualities that characterize a fluent action. A good grip and wrist action is mandatory for good rhythm. Of that I am certain. Equally, I am in no doubt that the quickest way to improve at this game is to work on creating good set-up habits that create the foundation to a good swing. I am flattered to be known around the world as a coach with a good grasp of swing mechanics, but what most people fail to realize is that, even with gifted players, I probably spend 90% of my time stressing the importance of the basics. Gravity, inertia, centrifugal force – all of those elements must be allowed to gel together in your swing to produce clubhead speed and force to meet the ball at impact. And no matter what your level of athleticism, adhering to golf's proven fundamentals is the one surefire key to making solid contact – and the more often you do that, the more you will enjoy playing this great game.

First things first...

A GOOD GRIP IS THE INSPIRATION BEHIND A GOOD SWING, AND ENABLES YOU TO HIT CONSISTENTLY STRAIGHT AND SOLID SHOTS

'*Good golf begins with a good grip.*' No less a figure than Ben Hogan declared that to the world at the height of his career, and, as in so many things, he was absolutely right. Your ability to get the clubhead *swinging* with any real momentum – and so create the clubhead speed that is necessary to hit solid shots – is really at the mercy of your grip. This coupling between you and the club must allow the hands to work together for the benefit of the swing, and compliment the motion of the wrists and arms and that of the body generally.

In other words, if a good swing synchronizes the swinging of the arms with the turning motion of your body, the grip is the vital go-between that passes on (and indeed enhances) that momentum via the shaft to the clubhead. It brings a swing to life.

Another pertinent lesson at this early stage is that the distance you are able to hit the ball is not all about physique and brute strength (though let there be no doubt that improving your levels of strength and flexibility will help your golf). It's the quality of the swing and the timing that lies within it that determines your ability to maximise your clubhead speed through impact and make solid contact – and again that boils down to the way the hands work together on the club. A good grip can be seen to multiply the

speed generated by the arms and body. So, on top of everything else, it's an important source of power.

As you read through all of the following sections of this book, I want you to be inquisitive and to feel free to experiment in just about every aspect… other than this one. There are certain things you can get away with in life, but one thing you cannot do is create (and, more importantly, expect to *repeat*) a good motion with a poor grip. A good grip is the inspiration behind a good swing, and enables you to hit consistently straight and solid shots; a poor one promises nothing but trouble.

• LEFT HAND HOLDS THE KEY •

It's not over-stating the scale of the problem to say that over 75% of the golfers that visit our teaching academies around the world arrive with a poor grip. And, of those (right handers), the majority struggle with the position of the left hand.

The problem is that golfers are prone to placing the club much too high in the palm of the left hand, to the extent that they threaten the mobility (hinge-ability, you might call it) of the left wrist. As a result they are simply unable to develop a hand action capable of transferring the full power of their swing through the shaft to the clubhead. One possible explanation for this could be that many players like to stand the club on the ground before they actually go about fitting the left hand on the grip, which automatically angles the grip high across the palm, up through the heel of the hand. To avoid this, my advice is that you try to get into the habit of holding the club up in front of your body, at about a 45 degree angle, and begin the process from there. Any time I'm working with a large group, and need what you might call a 'two-minute miracle', focusing on this position of the left hand and placing the club correctly in the fingers

virtually comes with a guarantee of success. That one small change makes an immediate difference to the feel a player has for the club and his ability to swing it freely. Think about it: The left hand is your first link with the club. Grip the club too high in the palm of the hand and you create a blockage that diminishes the ability to create a proper wrist cock, which reduces leverage. All this results in a player having to over-use the body or use the hands improperly (or a combination of both) in an attempt to find some power. That spells trouble for a golfer's distance, direction and consistency. And all because of a poor left hand grip.

So keep an eye on the position of your left hand. In fact, it's not a bad idea to draw a couple of lines on your glove as I have here to help you check that the shaft is running across the hand correctly. I really cannot stress this enough: place the club low in the hand, diagonally along the base of the fingers, and you will enjoy a greater wrist cock, more leverage, and generally hit more consistent and more solid shots with less effort. I've seen it a thousand times: this single adjustment to the position of the left hand will help to reduce a slice and increase distance.

The 'Two-minute' miracle

Focusing on the correct position of the left hand, and placing the club correctly in the fingers and palm – that's all it takes

· FIVE EASY STEPS TO A PERFECT GRIP ·

1 Holding the club up in front of your body, make sure the bottom (or 'leading') edge of the clubface is vertical to the horizon, pointing to 12 o'clock. Lay the grip in the fingers of your left hand, so that it runs from just below the base of your little finger all the way to the first joint of the forefinger.

2 Close your hand around the grip and squeeze gently with the last three fingers. You should be able to see between two and three knuckles on the back of the hand, while the left thumb and forefinger are 'snug' together.

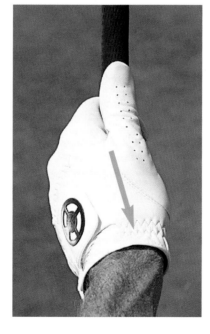

3 The 'line' that is seen to be formed between left thumb and knuckle should point in the direction of the right eye.

4 Spread the right hand so that as it joins the left, the club runs through the channel that is created at the base of the middle two fingers. When you close the right hand, the left thumb should disappear in that little 'cup' at the base of the right thumb. The 'line' on the right hand should now appear to run parallel to the 'line' on the left.

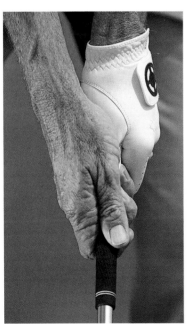

5 Finally, 'trigger' the right forefinger – i.e. crook it around the shaft so that it virtually meets the underside of the right thumb. You want your hands to be compact on the club, but don't squeeze too tightly; your grip pressure must at all times be sensitive to the weight of the clubhead.

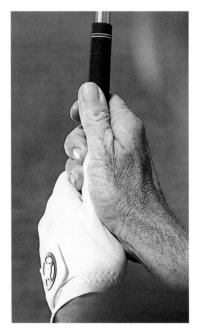

• A MARRIAGE OF CONVENIENCE •

The popular overlapping or 'Vardon' grip.

*A*bove all, your hands must be encouraged to work together as a unit. Neither one should dominate the other, and the quality of this union largely depends on how you choose to join the hands together. Basically, there are two principle grips in modern golf (three if you count the two-handed 'baseball' style which I regard as a good starter grip for juniors, and an alternative for ladies and seniors who may lack strength in the hands and arms).

You can either 'overlap' the little finger on the right hand on the forefinger of the left (some rest it in the channel between the first and second finger) or you can 'interlock' the right pinkie with the left forefinger.

Neither one of these styles is necessarily any better than the other. On balance, the overlapping grip is probably the most widely used on tour. It's all down to personal preference. Jack Nicklaus uses the interlocking grip and has done his entire career.

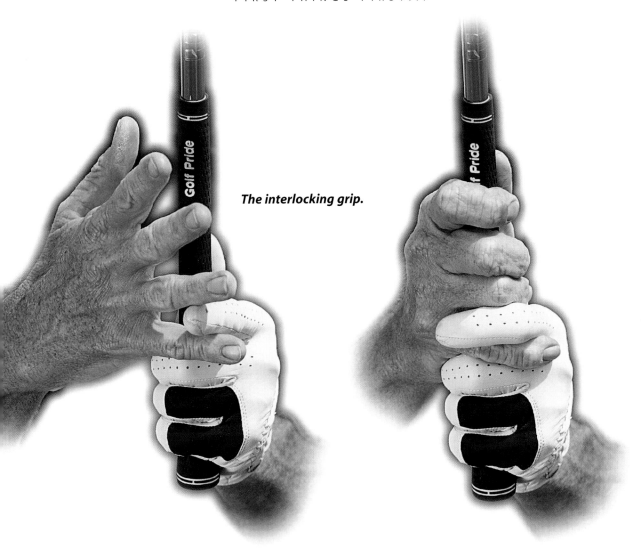

The interlocking grip.

Tiger Woods uses it. Other players prefer the feel of the overlapping (traditionally known as 'Vardon' after Harry Vardon) grip, which sees the pinkie on the right hand overlap the forefinger on the left.

Experiment with both to find the one that works best for you. Just be careful that if you do choose to interlock, you don't entwine your fingers too deeply, as that can lead to an excess of tension in the hands and wrists – and that ruins motion.

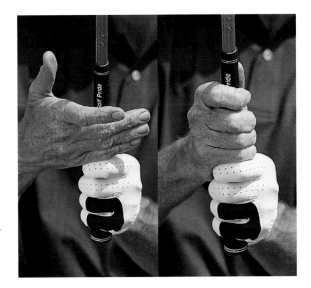

As an alternative, the 10-finger baseball-type grip may be utilized by players with weak hands – young juniors, seniors and ladies.

• FEEL IT…WAGGLE IT… 'SET' IT •

*H*ooking, or 'triggering', the right forefinger around the shaft (and at the same time separating it slightly from the middle finger) is a neat touch that immediately enhances your feel for the club-head and enlivens the hands to the prospect of making a swing. This 'trigger' also sees to it that the naturally stronger right hand (speaking for right-handed players) sits in a fairly passive position; rather than grab-bing the club like a hammer, you want to feel that you cradle it. This feature of your grip also makes a good 'waggle' of the club automatic as you instinctively move the clubhead about to keep the muscles in the hands and forearms supple.

For those of you not familiar with the term, a waggle refers to a small movement of the clubhead at the address position that is brought about by a small movement of the wrists and the forearms within the set-up position (right). And it serves at least two important functions: First, it helps to keep your hands and arms (and body gener-ally) relaxed and in motion. Second, properly rehearsed, the waggle gears the hands and forearms to work as they should in the first few feet

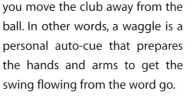

you move the club away from the ball. In other words, a waggle is a personal auto-cue that prepares the hands and arms to get the swing flowing from the word go.

Given that the majority of swing faults can be traced either to the set-up position, or some erratic first move, the importance of grooming these fundamentals should be crystal clear. There's no way round the fact that you need a good grip. Work on placing your hands together on the club and get used to the sensation of a good waggle. As you stand up to a ball, let your arms hang from the shoulders and keep those hands relaxed. Then let the hands lead the clubhead as they move laterally, a few inches back and forth.

What you want to feel here is that a gentle movement of the stomach is the stimulus that causes the hands to move the top of the club those few inches to the right and then back to the set-up, the clubhead following behind. At the same time you want to feel your weight *flow* back and forth between the feet as the whole body is keyed up, ready to move rather like a tennis player preparing to serve as he moves his body rhythmically in tandem with the bouncing of the ball.

This subtle movement of the body, arms and club is all designed to help you create the motion

necessary to make the swing. You can actually rehearse this without a club (see opposite). Stand in a good posture, your arms hanging from the shoulders, and initiate the lateral movement of the hands and arms with the centre of your body as you sway back and forth. As long as your hands remain free of tension you will soon have a sense of the way in which the relaxed muscles in the forearms get the clubhead moving smoothly away from the ball.

In the previous chapter I demonstrated how easy it is to get the clubhead swinging with just the thumb and first two fingers of the right hand on the grip. Now we have progressed to the point where we have the makings of a good swing with two hands on the club. Extending the waggle and adding to it a gentle turning motion of the upper body leads you naturally into a golf swing.

Look what happens: the wrists hinge (or 'set') and the club swings up on its way to the top. This is the completion of the backswing as far as the hands, arms and the club are concerned; now all you need to add is a full turn of the upper body. As you will discover in the following chapter, fully 'setting' the wrists to reach this halfway checkpoint is one of the milestones that I look for in the development of good technique. But we're getting ahead of ourselves.

HOW TO AIM THE CLUB
AND GET READY TO SWING

Think of a good grip as the essential coupling that allows you to swing the clubhead freely, and your set-up provides the necessary framework and foundation that enables you to turn your body effectively, to maintain good balance throughout, and – ultimately – to strike the ball towards your intended target. In other words it deals with the issues of alignment and posture, and the key here is that everything has to revolve around the clubface. Common sense, when you think about it. Every time you prepare to hit a shot, whether that's driving a ball off the tee or hitting a wedge to a green, the first thing you must do is make sure that the clubface looks at your target. To do that, you have to set the bottom edge (referred to as the 'leading edge') of the clubface squarely along the ball-to-target line. Once that is set in place, you are ready to complete your set-up.

*F*orming a grip is the first step in the process of preparing to swing a golf club, but I hope you'll agree that the lessons so far have not only given you the physical directions that you need to place your hands correctly, but also created images in your mind that enable you to conceptualize the basic shape of the swing itself. Now it's time to take things a stage further, and look in more detail at the way in which you set up to the ball in order to bring that swing to life.

Personal habits vary. Some players like to make their grip before they place the club behind the ball, others prefer to aim the club before completing their grip and settling down to the business of finalizing the posture. My advice to you is always to focus on getting your hands placed correctly on the grip before you think about aiming the clubface: take a moment to stand back from the ball and run through that process of fitting the hands with the club held up

in front of your body. Once satisfied with your grip, you can work on aiming the clubface at your target and completing your set-up with total confidence.

Whenever you intend to make a full swing, the rule of thumb is that you should stand with your feet, knees, hips and shoulders on a line that is parallel to the line of the shot – a position we describe as being 'square' to the target. Placing a couple of clubs on the ground will help you to recognise this when you practise. The fact that you are required to stand to the side of the ball can easily distort your perspective of a shot, but as soon as you create those parallel tracks you eliminate any uncertainty surrounding what good alignment both looks and feels like.

In terms of cementing the relationship between the alignment of the clubface and the position of your body, there's nothing to beat this practice routine: having made your grip, you simply aim the bottom edge of the clubface along the outer track, and then make sure that your body follows the inner track as you set about positioning your feet, knees, hips and shoulders in readiness to make your swing.

Finalizing the details of your posture most importantly involves bending from the hips to create this distinct spine angle, which provides the axis to your swing. Whether you are using a driver, a 5-iron or a wedge, the key is to stand up tall before flexing your knees and bending from the hips to ease your upper body forward. The lower part of your back should be comfortably straight (check this by holding a club against your spine), while the arms hang from the shoulders, placing the hands below the chin. Rehearse this sequence to galvanize the sensations of good posture, and check your angles in a mirror.

The neck should appear relaxed, tilting the head in such a way that your eyes look at the back of the ball. Your weight should be centred on the balls of your feet, while the lower body generally should feel 'springy', ready to stabilise the motion of the swing. As a rule of thumb you should feel a little 'connection' between your upper arms and your chest. And don't worry about how far you need to stand away from the ball. A good posture basically 'fits' every club; the length of the shaft will take care of that.

• FOLLOW-ME ROUTINES FOR POSTURE •

*I*sometimes refer to a good posture as a 'tall sit-down' position. That's really what you do: You stand up tall, then flex your knees as if you were about to sit down, and bend your upper body forwards until the sole of the club touches the ground. In the final analysis you should be in balance, ready to move, your body poised, knees flexed, eyes looking at the ball. Just be careful that you don't bend so far forwards that your weight is too much on the toes, or conversely stand so straight that your weight is too much on your heels.

(In a good posture you should quite easily find that you are able to rock gently back and forwards from the toes to the heels.) The moment you get your body out of balance at the set-up you will be forced into making compensations in your swing that will destroy your ability to strike the ball consistently. Remember, *for the club to swing in balance, your body has to be in balance.* That demands a good posture, one that is both comfortable and easy to repeat every time you step up to the ball.

● **Stand** up tall with your back straight, your feet shoulder-width apart, and place your hands on your hips. Use the inner track as your guide to the alignment of your feet, hips and shoulders.

● **Flex** your knees a little, as if you were about to sit down, and then gently push your hips back, so that you effectively stick your rear end out slightly, to create that angle between your upper and lower body.

● **Bring** the palms of your hands together with a clapping motion. Your arms should hang comfortably from the shoulders, with the hands beneath the chin.

● **Slide** the right hand down the left as if to make your grip, and check that your elbows look at the corresponding hip. There should now be a triangular look about the arms and shoulders.

FURTHER THOUGHTS ON STANCE
AND BALL POSITION

Now you have an understanding of the way in which you aim the club and stand to the ball, the next step is to apply these principles 'through the bag'. And this is where things start to get interesting, because now you have to think in terms of what you intend to achieve with your swing in order to hit the ball towards a specified target.

The visualization process subconsciously prepares you to make the right set-up: The moment you wrap your hands around a driver, your thoughts are geared towards sweeping the ball off a tee for a trajectory that maximizes distance; the more lofted clubs are all about accuracy, as you prepare to hit a controlled shot that lands the ball on the green. These themes are expanded further in chapter 3, where we will examine the characteristics behind some of the key shots in golf; for the time being, just be aware that the width of your stance, the position of the ball within it and relative distribution of your weight at the set-up are the chief elements that determine the nature of the strike on every shot.

Good balance is the making of every swing, and the width of your stance is obviously the No.1 consideration in this regard. For the driver, I like to see the feet spread to the width of the shoulders. No more. This provides you with all the stability you will ever need, while at the same time allowing you to turn and shift your weight in the course of making a full and powerful swing. As the length of the club shortens (and the loft increases), the swing naturally becomes more compact and controlled. Accordingly, the width of your stance should be seen to narrow a little (and it is only a little) as you work progressively through the irons towards the pitching clubs. We're only talking about an inch or so with every step down, but that's enough to make a difference to the character of the

shot you are intent on playing. I like to simplify the issue of ball position by suggesting that you think in terms of playing the ball forward in the stance (i.e. opposite the inside of the left heel) for the longer clubs (i.e. the driver and fairway woods), move it a little further back for the long- and mid-irons (3- to 7-iron), and play it approximately in the middle of the feet for the short irons (8-iron through wedge). This system is further simplified if you can get into the habit of relating the position of the ball to the position of your left heel. For many people I advise standing first with the feet close together, so that the ball position can easily be measured off in relation to the left heel before finally adjusting the width of the stance with the right foot.

A certain amount of trial and error will be required to find the combination of stance and ball position that best suits you. In the course of your experiments, you might also keep it in mind that many good players have favoured a system whereby they play the longer clubs from a slightly closed stance (i.e. the right foot is drawn back relative to the target line), square things up for the majority of the irons, and then open the stance slightly for the most lofted approach shots with the pitching clubs. The thinking behind this is that standing with the feet closed actively encourages a full turn of the upper body away from the target in the backswing, and so maximizes the coiling effect necessary for power. Opening up the stance (i.e. drawing the left foot back slightly) for the shortest irons is a common practice that simply gives you a better feel and stability for the shot, and helps you to release the club towards your target.

Study the three examples opposite (driver, 5-iron, 9-iron) to appreciate the extent of this variation in stance and ball position.

Driver:

Set up to a drive with the insides of your heels spread to the width of the shoulders. That gives you a good 'anchored' base. The ball should be played in the forward part of your stance, opposite the inside of the left heel. Here it is waiting to be 'collected' with an upward sweeping motion as the clubhead begins its ascent. Notice that the hands appear slightly behind the ball at address. That promotes the upward contact you are looking for with the least lofted club in the bag.

WEIGHT: *60:40 in favour of right side*
ALIGNMENT: *Feet square (or slightly closed) to the target line*

5-iron:

Moving down to a 5-iron, the stance narrows just a bit, perhaps by a couple of inches, the outsides of the feet now barely spread to the width of the shoulders. The ball is positioned a couple of inches inside the left heel, while my hands are now fractionally ahead of the club. This is a set-up designed to help you 'squeeze' the ball off the turf and leave only a shallow divot for the desired mid-iron trajectory.

WEIGHT: *Split 50:50 between the feet*
ALIGNMENT: *Feet parallel with the ball-to-target line*

9-iron:

The narrowest stance of all is reserved for the shorter and most lofted irons – but this base still provides good stability. The ball is now seen to be just about in the middle of the feet, and a useful check here is that it sits approximately in line with the buttons on your shirt. The hands are again ahead of the ball, and this position promotes the slightly descending ball-turf strike you are looking for with these clubs to control your approach shots with backspin.

WEIGHT: *40:60 in favour of left side*
ALIGNMENT: *Slightly open to the target line*

BALANCED POSTURE ALLOWS YOU TO 'SEQUENCE' YOUR SWING

Why do good players spend so much time and effort working on the details of their set-up and posture? Because this is the genesis of your game. This is a position that determines the living geometry of your swing – and your ability to repeat it. A good posture is the green light to using your body effectively and blending with it a free-flowing arm swing that enables you to accelerate the clubhead through the ball in the direction of your target. Your spine angle creates the axis about which the shoulders turn to create momentum; relaxed hands and arms are then responsible for establishing the rhythm with which you swing the clubhead.

Fundamental to my teaching philosophy is the importance of blending the arm-swing with the body turn, and once you have a good set-up in place you can begin to experience what I like to describe as the proper 'sequencing' of your swing. By that, I mean you

can think about synchronizing the movement of the arms with the turning of the body, and the exercise you see below will help you to appreciate the way these components gel together.

You can rehearse this anywhere: Place your left hand on your chest, just below the chin, and adopt a good posture, hanging your right arm comfortably, the palm of the hand facing an imaginary target. Then, in slow motion, make a swing, and focus on the quality of the timing that exists between the rotation of your body and the swinging of that right arm.

The key to this exercise is that your turn and your arm-swing match-up; in other words, the sequence of your swing should be such that the right hand reaches the top of the backswing as you complete your turn away from the target, arrives at impact as your body unwinds and clears before finally catching up once more at the finish. As the quality of your timing improves you will find you can actually get quite vigorous in this, winding and then unwinding your body to accelerate the right arm through impact.

What you are developing is the 'gearing' effect. The outer part of your swing (arms and hands) and the inner part of the swing (your body, the hub) work 'in sync'; translated to the mechanics of your swing, this results in the speed generated by the rotary motion of your body being multiplied through the natural arc of your arm-swing all the way down to the clubhead.

Sequencing your swing in this way is critical in terms of the speed you generate at impact. I see a lot of players who move their body quickly, but have no clubhead speed to show for it. Because there is no dynamic motion present, the club and body move at pretty much the same speed. Other players appear to move their body very slowly, but create terrific clubhead speed at impact – where it's needed most. This explains why you find many slightly built players who, pound for pound, are out there with the big hitters; they create leverage and utilize centrifugal forces to multiply their body speed and accelerate the clubhead at a fantastic rate.

What you have to remember here is that your body doesn't hit the ball; the clubhead does. And the better you rotate your body and synchronize with it the swinging of the arms and the hands, the more clubhead speed you will create.

• HOW TO RUN YOUR SWING ON AUTOMATIC •

Though it may only last a matter of seconds, a pre-shot routine is critical in terms of your ability to repeat a good swing. And the more you practise these simple tasks (i.e. establishing a good grip, aim, posture and so on) the more doing so will become automatic. That's the irony of golf; you practise so that you can forget. In this regard, a pre-shot routine is also your first line of defence against pressure. Focusing your mind on a series of simple tasks gives you something positive to work on in the moments leading up to the shot itself. Rather than worrying about your swing, or what might happen as a consequence of a poor shot, you simply run through a disciplined series of 'pre-flight' safety measures that take good care of the fundamentals. Your mind is constructive, not destructive.

When people ask what's the difference between good and great players (and this could even explain the difference between a mid-teen handicap and a single figure player), it's usually the quality of the preparation before a shot that holds the answer. It's about taking care of the basics, and if you get nothing more out of this book than learning how to grip the club and set up to the ball correctly, you will be a better golfer for it. Believe me, I can spot a good player from the far end of the range by the way he or she goes about the basics – aiming the club, making the grip and standing to the ball.

A slick routine suggests to me that a player is in control of his actions, that he is thinking clearly, that he is focused on the shot. This is something you have to develop. One of the fascinations of watching the pro's in action is to observe the various mannerisms that characterize individual styles on the course. That's another quirk of this game. While we learn the same lessons and play from pretty much the same script, we're all very different as golfers.

Remember, most faults in the swing occur in the moments leading up to the action, so developing and working on the details of your own pre-shot routine is the obvious way to prevent careless mistakes creeping into your game. In closing this chapter, let me summarize the key points that I want you to concentrate on by way of a typical pre-shot routine. According to the yardage book, I have 160 yards to the middle of the green, and (as usual) I'm better off getting the ball right up to the hole than being short. There's a breeze off the right, and I reckon it's a comfortable 7-iron shot for me. Here goes…

● **Start** your routine behind the ball to get a good look at the shot you are about to play. Focus on the target, and try to get a picture in your mind of the ball flying towards it. As you do this, hold the club up and make your grip. Get your hands comfortably placed on the shaft and keep those arms 'soft'.

● **Retain** that image of the shot in your mind and walk around in a circle so that you approach the ball face on, taking care to aim the bottom edge of the club squarely at your target. When you are happy with your aim, create your stance and ball position, making sure your body is parallel to the line of the shot.

● **Swivel** your head to allow your eyes to focus on the target, and as you do so keep your hands, arms and body in continuous motion with a gentle back-and-forth waggle of the clubhead. With one final glance at the target, pull the trigger, and let the shot unfold – just as you pictured it in your mind.

CHAPTER

Putting a swing together...

**USE THESE LESSONS TO FEEL THE 'LINKS'
THAT SHAPE THE BASIC SWING, AND THEN BLEND THEM
TOGETHER WITH RHYTHM**

*C*onfusion. That's what holds most golfers back. Because this game has a reputation for being difficult, otherwise relaxed and well adjusted individuals have a tendency to want to think too much the moment they pick up a golf club. And when things don't work out the way they intended, what happens? They think even harder about what they are doing. One of the great expressions you often hear applied to players who fall into this trap is that he or she suffers 'paralysis through analysis' – i.e. they get so caught up thinking about the swing they have no hope of making one. I've seen it a thousand times. The brain gets in the way.

This mental 'interference' can be explained, at least in part, by the fact that golf revolves around a stationary ball. In just about every other game you care to mention, a player's movement is more of a *reflexive* action. There simply isn't the time to think about how to react; whether swinging a tennis racket or a baseball bat, when the ball comes your way you have a split-second to deal with it, and your response is virtually automatic. But in golf it's up to you to initiate the motion. And, just to make things more interesting, the nature of the game is such that you have all the time in the world in between shots to think about doing so.

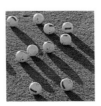

The mental challenge this poses is without doubt one of the biggest hurdles to overcome in learning to play with any degree of success. And this tendency golfers have to over-complicate the business of making a swing only reinforces my belief that the best way to teach one is to give away as little information as possible. While we teachers might like to think that once in a while we come up with something radical and new, the fact is the swing revolves around a few basic ground rules that are as old as the game itself. The harmony of a good swing has its origins in the set-up position, and now that you have a grounding in those fundamentals, my intention in this chapter is to familiarize you with a series of key checkpoints that will enable you to be your own best coach in putting a good swing together.

• HOW TO MAKE BEST USE OF THESE LESSONS •

Many of my students are surprised when I say this, but you really can develop the basis of a good swing away from the course, either at home or in the office. Certainly in the initial stages of learning, I am a great believer in practising swing technique and grooving a few positions or 'links' in the swing *without the distraction of hitting a ball*. The split-hands exercise that you are about to experience will enable you to do just that.

What I am about to teach you is not some watered down theory for the mass market but the basis of the instruction all of my students get to learn. And it's really not complicated at all. If you distill the swing into its simplest form, it's a turning motion of the body accompanied by the free and easy swinging of the arms, along with a wrist action that enables you to keep the swing flowing – all resulting in the clubface being square and travelling at maximum speed at impact. The set-up position creates the angles that determine a good swing; all you have to

do is trust them. If there is a secret to playing good golf it is in learning to synchronize the movement of the arms and the body, and then to repeat the motion with good rhythm. Identifying with each of the following positions will help you to do just that, and with a little practice (even if that involves swinging a club only periodically in the back garden), this chapter will reward you with a sound structure to build on.

As you may have already noticed, I am not holding the club with a regular grip. My hands are a couple of inches apart, and, as you are about to discover, separating them in this fashion heightens your sensation of each move to create a terrific learning experience. The split-grip drill also emphasizes the function of a good wrist hinge in the swing; with the hands separated, all the fingers are on the grip, and you really do get a sense of cocking the left hand and hingeing the right wrist as you 'set' the club in the backswing to establish the leverage that accelerates the club in the downswing. All of the following positions are important, but pay special attention to this 'set' position halfway back. That really holds the key to your consistency at the top of the backswing.

The trick is to work on 'layering' these links one on top of the other; by that, I mean to build your swing up gradually, and always return to the set-up position at the start of each new sequence. As you become more familiar with each of these positions you will find that you are able to swing the clubhead through them almost without thinking. Once the swing is started correctly, with the hands, arms and body working 'together' to give you that initial momentum, the backswing and throughswing movement is essentially a chain reaction, each 'link' leading you on to the next. The underlying theme throughout this section is that *a good swing is a continuous flowing motion* – don't threaten its course by overloading your brain with too many technical thoughts.

Perfect posture gets you ready to go

Good teaching will always stress the importance of golf's fundamentals. That way you prepare to create a chain reaction from a balanced starting point. Pick up a mid iron, assume a good posture and then slide your right hand down the shaft about 2 inches or so, until the trigger unit of the right hand is on the metal, to create the grip I am using here. Flex your knees, so that you feel springy on your feet, and as you settle into position make sure that your right side sinks a little lower than the left (this includes having your right arm set lower than the left). It's important that you have this slant across the shoulders, and you should be aware also of the upper part of each arm resting lightly on your chest (that promotes good 'connection'). Hold onto the club lightly, so that your forearms are relaxed, and look for this triangular relationship between the arms and shoulders as you extend the club comfortably in front of your body.

• MAKING THE FIRST MOVE •

Start your arms and the club away 'together'

To get the motion underway you have to get it synchronized from the start – and that flowing quality has its origins in the start back, or moveaway. And the key is to focus on maintaining the shape of that triangle as you move the club to the right, thus maintaining the symmetry between the club, arms and shoulders until your hands pass close to the right thigh. Make it a one-piece move to this first checkpoint, where the butt-end of the club points at your middle, and the clubhead points to about 8 o'clock on an imaginary clock-face (6 o'clock being the ball).

Repeat this motion back and forth, returning to the set-up position before again making this first move. Try to sense the general momentum of the swing as it begins to work away from the target: your stomach will want to go with the flow and your weight will begin to shift towards the right foot. Everything about this first move is designed to get this momentum going, the hands, arms and body working away from the target 'together'. The hands and forearms remain passive, the wrists have yet to hinge (they are about to do so), but the swing is started off on the right track, the clubhead working naturally inside the ball-to-target line.

When you hold the club with a regular grip you will soon appreciate the way in which a good waggle of the clubhead primes the swing: the hands, forearms and shoulders work as a well-oiled unit to get the clubhead started on the right track. To think in terms of getting the butt-end of the club moving before the clubhead helps some players to achieve this lateral look away from the ball (see chapter 5 – Simple Reminders); another useful swing thought here is that as your left shoulder turns it pushes the left arm down slightly, so that the hands pass close to the right thigh, and the clubhead remains low to the ground as it moves back on the inside.

Maintain the triangle shape between arms and shoulders as you get the swing underway.

• HALFWAY BACK •

Wrists hinge to get the club swinging up on plane

I promised in the introduction to this book that swing theory would appear on a strictly 'need-to-know' basis. Well, here's something I believe every golfer needs to familiarize himself with and learn to understand: *a good wrist action is essential in terms of creating a repeating motion and maximizing your clubhead speed through the ball.* If you watch the pro's swing these days you will see that most of them have their wrists fully cocked (or 'set') by the time the left arm reaches parallel, and that angle is then retained deep into the downswing, until the centrifugal forces created by the body cause the angle to 'snap' and the clubhead is accelerated into the back of the ball.

Having started the club, arms and the chest away together, the next link in the chain sees the wrists hinge to swing the club up to this halfway checkpoint. The split-hands grip accentuates the move perfectly: building on the momentum created in the move-away, as the left arm continues to swing across the chest, the right elbow folds comfortably and the right hand hinges back on itself to

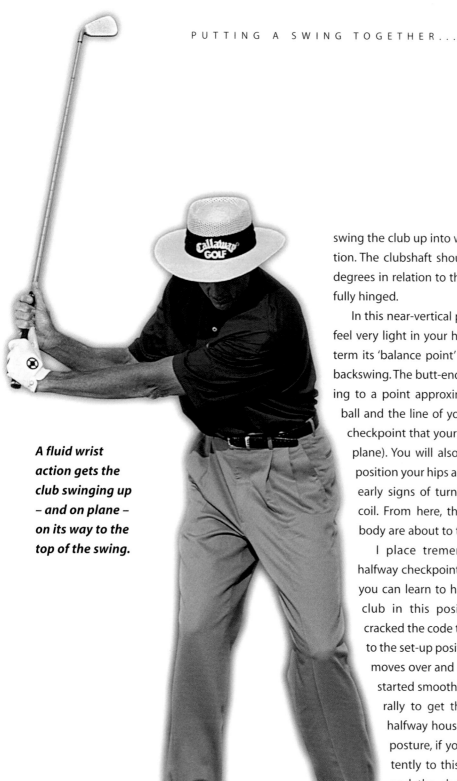

A fluid wrist action gets the club swinging up – and on plane – on its way to the top of the swing.

swing the club up into what we term a fully 'set' position. The clubshaft should now be seen to be at 90 degrees in relation to the left arm, and the wrists are fully hinged.

In this near-vertical position, the club should now feel very light in your hands – it has found what we term its 'balance point' on its way to the top of the backswing. The butt-end of the club should be pointing to a point approximately midway between the ball and the line of your feet (this is a pretty good checkpoint that your swing is on a good path and plane). You will also notice that in reaching this position your hips and shoulders are showing the early signs of turning to create the backswing coil. From here, the big muscles in the upper body are about to take over.

I place tremendous importance on this halfway checkpoint, for the simple reason that if you can learn to hinge your wrists and 'set' the club in this position you have pretty well cracked the code to a good backswing. Go back to the set-up position and rehearse these initial moves over and over again, getting the swing started smoothly until the wrists hinge naturally to get the club swinging up to this halfway house. Assuming a good grip and posture, if you can swing the club consistently to this point, with a full wrist cock and the shaft up on plane, completing your upper body movement with a full turn of the shoulders will reward you with a solid backswing, ready to unwind into the ball.

• AT THE TOP •

Fully turned, fully 'coiled'

And here's the proof. From the halfway 'set' checkpoint, it's simply a matter of completing your shoulder turn over the resistance of a flexed and braced right knee to achieve this coiled position at the top of the backswing. The left shoulder turns under the chin, and your back faces the target. It's important that the right elbow is not tucked in to the side of the body, but that it swings out freely to create this symmetry with the left arm at the top, where it supports the club beautifully. You have turned your upper body about the natural axis provided by the spine, and the arms have swung up accordingly.

As you arrive at this fully 'loaded' position you should be aware of some tension in the lower part of your torso as the muscles are stretched. You have turned your shoulders through at least 90 degrees, the hips through about 45. In other words, you have 'coiled' your upper body against a resisting lower half. Let your left heel come up off the ground a bit only if that's necessary for you to achieve this full turn. Otherwise I advise keeping the feet flat on the ground, and all movement in the

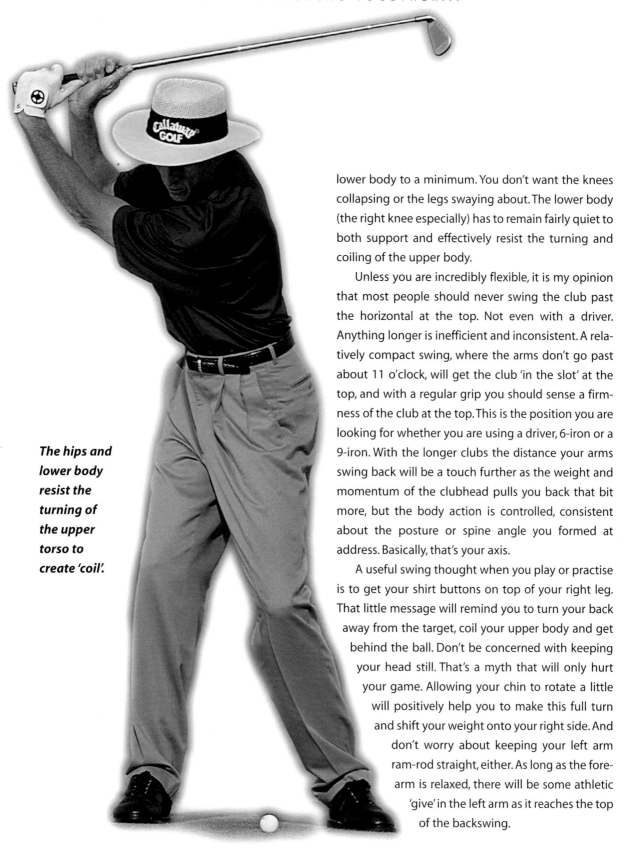

The hips and lower body resist the turning of the upper torso to create 'coil'.

lower body to a minimum. You don't want the knees collapsing or the legs swaying about. The lower body (the right knee especially) has to remain fairly quiet to both support and effectively resist the turning and coiling of the upper body.

Unless you are incredibly flexible, it is my opinion that most people should never swing the club past the horizontal at the top. Not even with a driver. Anything longer is inefficient and inconsistent. A relatively compact swing, where the arms don't go past about 11 o'clock, will get the club 'in the slot' at the top, and with a regular grip you should sense a firmness of the club at the top. This is the position you are looking for whether you are using a driver, 6-iron or a 9-iron. With the longer clubs the distance your arms swing back will be a touch further as the weight and momentum of the clubhead pulls you back that bit more, but the body action is controlled, consistent about the posture or spine angle you formed at address. Basically, that's your axis.

A useful swing thought when you play or practise is to get your shirt buttons on top of your right leg. That little message will remind you to turn your back away from the target, coil your upper body and get behind the ball. Don't be concerned with keeping your head still. That's a myth that will only hurt your game. Allowing your chin to rotate a little will positively help you to make this full turn and shift your weight onto your right side. And don't worry about keeping your left arm ram-rod straight, either. As long as the forearm is relaxed, there will be some athletic 'give' in the left arm as it reaches the top of the backswing.

· STARTING DOWN ·

Unwind your body, accelerate the clubhead

Earlier I talked about 'layering' these moves one on top of the other to get a real sense of the way each of these links in the swing blends into the next. Well, here is where the benefit of that process will really hit home: in the change of direction.

The true dynamics of a good swing are revealed in the split-second a player begins to unwind. Blending the two halves of the swing efficiently is often talked about as the most important move in golf: As you reach the top of your backswing, you are at the same time starting down – i.e. the left heel is re-planted, the left hip pulls back towards the target, and the momentum is reversed. And, as the body unwinds, the arms and hands follow suit, and the club drops on to a shallow delivery

Having coiled your body up like a spring, releasing that energy accelerates the clubhead on its way towards impact.

plane, ready to accelerate the clubhead squarely into the back of the ball.

The secret to understanding the dynamics of this move is to build up the backswing in stages, and use the energy in the fully coiled position to feel your way into the downswing. As you wind up, coiling your upper body and transferring your weight on to that braced right knee, you are creating a momentum which is enhanced and accelerated as you change direction. Rehearse this in a mini sequence: get to the top and start down. Back to the top and start down. Groove the move. From the top of the swing, try to feel the change of direction from the ground up: your weight returns to the left foot, the left hip rotates back towards the target and the upper body follows suit. Having created a powerful coil in the backswing, as your body unwinds the arms drop the club into this hitting position, the wrists still fully hinged and loaded with energy, ready to strike the ball. *Don't forcibly pull the arms down, let them fall as the right elbow works down adjacent to the right hip.*

We talk about the swing being a chain reaction, and nowhere is it more so than in this sequence from the top. The big danger that you have to be aware of is being impatient, rushing the changeover and trying to force the club down. You have to resist that urge to lunge with your body at the ball. Let the motion unfold naturally as gravity takes over. When you ask good players what they do to hit the ball harder, most will say that they try to complete the backswing and start down slowly. What they mean is they make an effort to make this transition as fluid as possible in order to preserve the coil and maximize the acceleration through impact. They swing easy, but hit hard.

· IMPACT ·

Feel the forces at work

The most important thing to understand about impact is that it is a position you swing through at high speed. It's a moment in a sequence. Gone. Impact happens so quickly that this is not something you can consciously try to control. It's a position that comes about as a result of the chain reaction you have created – starting with the set-up, and accelerated through a good transition from the top of the backswing. The quality of impact depends on the quality of your swing.

Having said that, I do believe it is important to understand the nature of a good impact position. And the first point to note here is that the spine angle that was established at address has been maintained right up to the moment the club strikes the back of the ball. That provides you with a consistent axis about which to turn and thus make a repeating swing (note that as you release the club through impact you will naturally begin to straighten your body as you complete your finish).

Good players control the rotation of their body to return the arms, hands and clubface squarely to the ball – pretty much the position they assumed at address. As

you see, the hips and shoulders are open to the target, while the left side of the body is 'braced' to absorb the hit (hence the expression 'hit into a firm left side'). The left wrist is flat and slightly bowed, while the angle at the back of the right hand is held. The image is that the left arm and the shaft form a straight line; this is where you want to get your left arm straight – nowhere else.

Motion is of the essence. What you want to experience here is a free-wheeling acceleration through the ball as the centrifugal forces at work pull your hands and arms towards the target. Obviously the longer the club you are using, the more speed you will create, but the motion with every club is the same. When you unwind correctly, the right side of your body will enjoy the freedom to power through the shot, keep the club accelerating and fire the ball towards the target. When you practise, stop every now and then and push the clubhead against something firm to get a sense of what a good impact feels like. But when you return to hitting balls, focus on swinging *through* the shot. Let the ball get in the way.

The body angles that were created at the set-up are maintained right up to the point of impact, as the clubhead returns squarely to the ball.

· THROUGH THE BALL ·

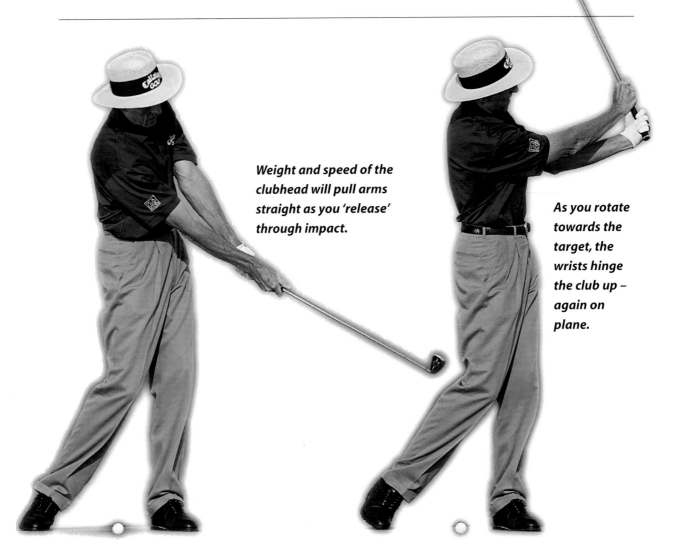

Weight and speed of the clubhead will pull arms straight as you 'release' through impact.

As you rotate towards the target, the wrists hinge the club up – again on plane.

Body rotates, arms fully released

The symmetry that exists in a good swing is again evident in the moments after impact, as the arms release the clubhead towards the chosen target. You are running on automatic from this point and onwards, free-wheeling through these positions on the way to the finish.

As a result of the centrifugal forces at work, when you swing for real the clubhead will pull the arms straight immediately after impact; with your hands split apart on the grip, you are looking for the triangular shape between the arms and the shoulders that you originally established at address.

This is basically a mirror image of the 8 o'clock moveaway position in the backswing, albeit with rather more body motion as you are now unwinding in the direction of the target. From here, the right hand and right forearm naturally turn over the left to swing the club up once more on

Finish with the right shoulder pointing at the target, body straight up-and-down.

Through and beyond impact the uncoiling of the body is complete – the body is perfectly balanced.

plane on its way to the final follow through position. Again, the split-hands grip accentuates that sensation of turning the right hand over the left to a virtual mirror image of the halfway 'set' position in the backswing. The majority of your weight is now across into the left side of your body, supported by a braced left leg, with both the hips and the upper body now rotated towards the target.

A good, committed release of the clubhead will lead you all the way to the finish – the final link in the chain. And the important thing here is that you have done just that – finished. Your body has rotated all the way through the shot, so that you end up with your right shoulder facing the target, eyes forward, club wrapped in balance behind your neck. Make this a trademark: Round it all off with a classically poised position, your body relatively straight, weight fully on the left side.

A good player rotates his body and accelerates freely through the ball; poor players are prone to hit at the ball and often cut their follow through short as a result of deceleration. Don't fall into that trap. The key is to build speed gradually from the top of the backswing and flow the clubhead all the way to a full and balanced finish – a position you should be able to hold for several seconds.

• FULL SWING EXERCISES •

Now you have the moves, it's time to add the motion

Now that you are familiar with the basic shape of the swing, it's time to work on fusing these individual moves together to create a continuous flowing motion. Working on specific positions – *and repeating them often* – will give you a glimpse of the chain reaction we are trying to develop, but when it comes to the end product you don't want to be standing on the golf course thinking in bits and pieces. Learning these links will give you a sound basic shape to work with; now it's time to give your swing some substance – to lubricate it, if you will, and give it a rhythm and a flow that brings it to life.

Learning a swing is in many ways like learning to dance. Now you have the steps, it's time to turn on the music. The key is to find what makes your swing tick. Tempo, for one thing, is a very personal quality. The overall speed at which you turn and swing the club must be allowed to reflect your character. My good friend Nick Price is a bundle of energy; everything is *go, go go*, and that's the way he swings the golf club. A couple of waggles, and bang! It's gone. Tiger Woods is deliberate, but very aggressive. Ernie Els is the exact opposite. Ernie is laid back, he's never hurried, and his swing is effortless. Vijay Singh swings it easy, too. Different tempos all of them, but superb ball strikers every one. And what you must understand is that this natural tempo runs right the way through the bag, from the driver to the irons and to the putter. This is what makes them consistent.

The following drills will help you to capitalise on this notion of synchronizing the movement of the arms and the body. Work on them in conjunction with the split-hands exercise to develop the quality of your motion. When you get to the point of hitting balls, make it easier on yourself and tee balls up, even with the irons. And remember, good players don't hit 'at' the ball, they simply let it get in the way of the swinging clubhead. Think in terms of 'collecting' the ball off the tee and you will give yourself a much better chance of hitting some quality shots – and that will do wonders for your confidence.

Turn on the style for a better body action (and more power)

Placing a club behind your shoulders and rehearsing this pivot motion is one of the best exercises you can do to develop the heart of your swing – i.e. the turning motion of the torso. Good players generate power with a turning motion that sees the upper body coiled against the resistance of a solid lower body action. This exercise will put the same quality in your swing. The more you do this, the more you will learn to rotate your shoulders on a consistent plane, and the more that will promote swinging the club around your body on an arc (or track) that ensures the clubhead approaches impact on the correct path and angle. (Note: if it feels more comfortable, hooking the club in your elbows behind your lowerback is just as effective as placing it across the shoulders.)

The first thing to check as you take hold of the club and assume a good posture is that you create this distinct tilt across the shoulders, the left shoulder and left hip slightly higher than the right side. That sets your upper body in the perfect position. As you get ready to make your move, pull gently with both hands to flex the shaft and prepare your muscles for a

work-out. To start the backswing motion, turn your left shoulder under your chin until the butt-end of the club points behind (and slightly beyond) the ball. Feel your chest and back muscles *turning, stretching and winding*. The key is to sense that you turn against the resistance of that flexed right knee as you literally wind up your backswing. Hold this stretched position for a few seconds: your hips have now turned through approximately 45

Success guaranteed

Use the pivot drill as a warm-up exercise before you play, and strengthen the very heart of your swing

degrees, the shoulders a full 90. The majority of your weight should be into your right side, and your upper body feels 'coiled' against the lower half. From here you want to feel that the energy stored in that backswing position unwinds your body all the way to a full finish, your body now fairly straight up and down, the right shoulder pointing at the target, and your weight now balanced on your left side, left leg firm.

Turn the shoulders through a full 90 degrees (both back and through), and feel the 'stretch' in the torso.

Repeat this as often as you can. Not only will this drill reward you with a strong body motion (the core of every good swing) but it's a terrific stretching exercise that will help to keep your body supple. Just

be careful that as you complete the backswing the butt-end of the clubshaft points slightly beyond the ball; if it should point at (or slightly inside) the ball, the chances are you are tilting your shoulders which will

prevent you ever getting your weight fully behind the ball in the backswing. Turn and shift your weight about the axis created by your spine angle. Try to maintain that angle from the set-up all the way to the moment of impact, and don't worry if your head has to move a little to accommodate a full turn away from the ball. Virtually every dynamic swing features lateral head movement.

Build it up, let the clubhead find its way…

For me, the wonderful thing about working on a good posture and gripping the club lightly, so that the hands and forearms remain relaxed, is that once the swing gets underway the clubhead really dictates the line it swings on. And if you study the images of a good swing you will see that the natural positions in the backswing are reflected almost perfectly in the through-swing. There's a terrific symmetry as you wind and unwind, and the exercise you see here is designed to build on the notion that the clubhead virtually swings itself as long as you are prepared to let the motion *flow.*

Layer each move one on top of the other, and build up the shape and the rhythm of a repeating swing.

To enjoy this experience, get yourself set-up to the ball, and then extend your arms and the club forward into this quarter-through starting position. From here, let the clubhead fall and in one continuous motion swing it back to the 8 o'clock position. Then reverse the momentum once more and swing through to halfway. Then let the clubhead fall once more, this time to the fully 'set' position in the back-swing. Build up your momentum as you match these mirror images: quarter-to-quarter, half-to-half. With each repetition you will develop your sense of the hands and arms sychnronizing their motion with the turning of the body, and also you will become very aware of the rhythm of your swing. Build up to a full swing and hit shots with this drill – just remember to tee the ball up and 'collect' it through impact.

Start the club forward, and then pick up the action as you let it fall in one continuous motion.

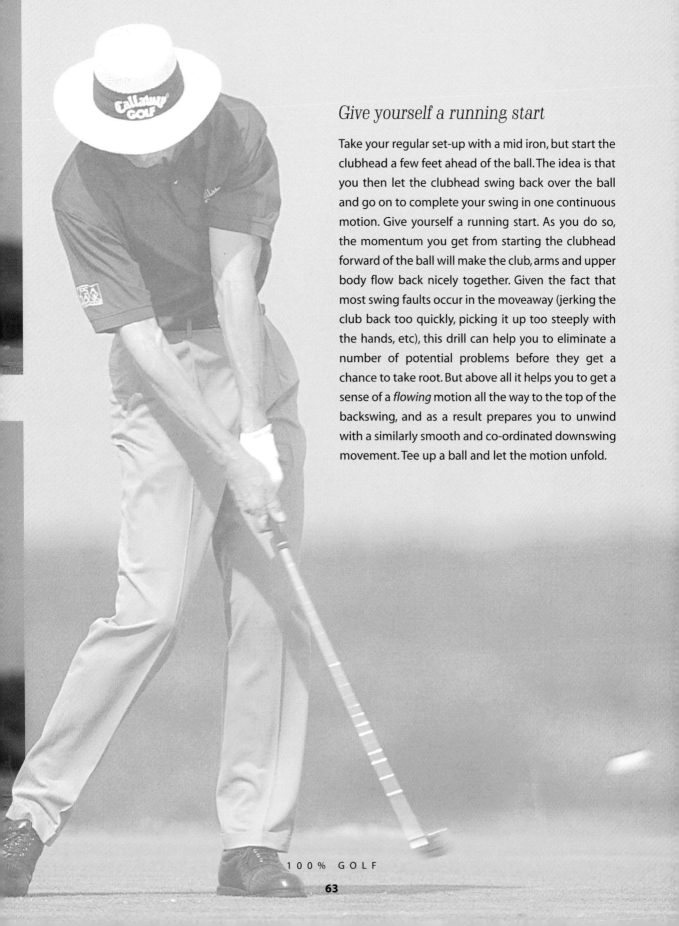

Give yourself a running start

Take your regular set-up with a mid iron, but start the clubhead a few feet ahead of the ball. The idea is that you then let the clubhead swing back over the ball and go on to complete your swing in one continuous motion. Give yourself a running start. As you do so, the momentum you get from starting the clubhead forward of the ball will make the club, arms and upper body flow back nicely together. Given the fact that most swing faults occur in the moveaway (jerking the club back too quickly, picking it up too steeply with the hands, etc), this drill can help you to eliminate a number of potential problems before they get a chance to take root. But above all it helps you to get a sense of a *flowing* motion all the way to the top of the backswing, and as a result prepares you to unwind with a similarly smooth and co-ordinated downswing movement. Tee up a ball and let the motion unfold.

Two clubs tell one story

Here's another good exercise to further illustrate (and test) the shape and the plane of your swing. It also gives you great visual feedback in front of a mirror. What you do is grip a club in each hand and focus on maintaining about a six inch gap between the two shafts as you prepare to swing them to the top of the backswing (this is a better backswing than downswing drill).

As you swing the club back you will find that you create this six inch band of plane, which is easier to observe than a single shaft. And that visual imagery helps you to get the plane of your swing on track.

Rehearsing your backswing motion will teach you how the right arm and the left arm work both independently and together in the course of a making a good backswing. The key is to swing in slow motion, and feel the two hands working in sync, tracking one another as you maintain that relationship between the two clubs. Be warned, however, that this drill simply doesn't tolerate one hand working independently of the other – the shafts will end up clashing if that happens. So use this exercise to get the left hand and the right hand working together in tandem.

Enhance the shape of your swing

I like to think of the right arm as the guiding arm in a good swing: allowed to swing freely, it gives you a good sense of width going back, and establishes the position of the club at the top of the back-swing as the elbow folds. Then, in the changeover, allowing the right elbow to fall towards the right hip is a sure sign that you 'shallowed' out the plane of your downswing in readiness for impact, where-upon the right hand whips through the ball. Swinging a club with your right arm only develops the quality of this action generally, and enhances the outline of a good swing. (Note: If you struggle to control the weight of the clubhead, turning the club around and swishing the grip is just as effective.)

Take a short iron and assume your normal set-up position, but go down a little with the right hand for extra feel and control. Sense the weight of the clubhead on the end of the shaft and then go ahead and swing it to feel exactly what the right arm is doing. Immediately you should be aware of swinging the clubhead

away from the ball to establish good width and a natural radius to your swing. Then, as the right hand hinges back on itself and the elbow folds comfortably, the club swings up to the top. The check-point I look for here is that the underside of the right arm is paral-lel with the ground, the right hand now fully hinged back on itself, and the shaft is parallel with the ball-to-target line.

Check your backswing posi-tion a couple of times and then make a full swing. As you change direction (and this needs to hap-pen as smoothly and effortlessly as possible) you want to sense that the right elbow falls towards the right hip before the arm straightens and accelerates the clubhead through impact. If you feel confident enough to give it a go, tee up a ball and hit a few shots with a short iron. Placing the ball on a tee will encourage you to swing freely through impact and not hit at the ball. That quality is really what this drill is designed to teach you, and the momentum you create will take you all the way to a full and balanced finish.

Swing to a regular beat

Here's a long-time classic that will quickly improve the overall rhythm and tempo of your swing: practise with your feet close together, no more than three or four inches apart. Take a mid- to short iron and spend

just a few minutes clipping balls off a tee-peg. In no time at all this will blend the free swinging of the arms with the controlled rotary motion of the body.

The reason this drill is so effective is that on such a narrow stance you cannot possibly over-use your body. That's the real benefit here. If you hurry from the

top, you will lose your balance. With your feet close together, the emphasis is on turning the body and swinging your arms in harmony. When you get the blend of arms and body just right, you will enjoy a sense of calmness as you start down, and start striking the ball right out of the middle of the clubface.

As a warm-up drill, you should also make use of this exercise before a game, lopping the tops off daisies if you don't have the time to hit balls. In my teaching I continually emphasize blending the arm swing with the turning motion of the body, and this drill backs me up perfectly.

Enjoy more speed
with the baseball move

With a club held up in front of your body, it's amazing just how freely and instinctively you begin to swing. That's why I'm a firm believer in the benefits of the baseball drill: it quickly helps you to co-ordinate the movement of club and body, and in a short space of time teaches you to maximize your velocity through the hitting area with a loud swish. Swinging a club baseball style is also a terrific way to increase your

clubhead speed. When you hold the club out at waist high, you automatically seem to turn your upper body much more effectively, and the result is that you make a better coil and release – i.e. you load up your backswing and unwind with more speed and power. It also helps anyone with a tendency to swing from out-to-in. Holding the club up at this angle gives you a much better sense of swinging the club around your body, moving inside back to square and inside once more on the way through.

Ideally for most golfers, this will help produce a draw shaped shot, one that moves right to left in the air – a far cry from the left to right slice shape that costs distance and accuracy. So use this drill to up your speed and at the same time to get the feel for the shape and the path of your golf swing. Make swings out in front of you, and lower the clubhead in stages until you are ready to strike a ball off a tee. As you simplify your mechanics, so your shots will become longer and more on line.

CHAPTER

Key shots every golfer must learn

**WITH MINOR ADJUSTMENTS TO THE SET-UP,
YOUR BASIC SWING SHAPE CAN BE APPLIED TO
EVERY CLUB IN THE BAG**

*B*ack in the 1930s and 1940s when big-time professional golf was beginning to take off on both sides of the Atlantic, the leading players of the day were offered a fee to carry and endorse the equipment of the various manufacturers. It was an unrestricted practice, and not uncommon for a player to have twenty clubs or more in his golf bag – half of which he probably never touched. To the relief of caddies everywhere, the rules were changed in 1938, when the United States Golf Association determined that the maximum number of clubs in a full set should be limited to 14 (the Royal & Ancient Golf Club at St Andrews followed suit in 1939).

The make-up of a full set hasn't changed that much down the years, although modern technology has certainly come a long way to benefit everyone who plays the game, particularly with the lighter and stronger titanium heads that you find in drivers and fairway metals. Increasingly, though, what you do find is a tendency among professionals to substitute one or two of the traditional long irons (i.e. the 1-, 2- and even 3-iron) for what has become known in the business as a 'utility' wood (i.e. a small-headed and lofted fairway wood) that is generally more forgiving than a long iron, particularly out of a poor lie. Most good players these days also like to carry at least two or

three wedges of varying degrees of loft to provide the versatility for a wide range of feel shots around the green. More on that in chapter 4.

Choosing the equipment to suit your own playing characteristics is a vital first step for anyone serious about the game, and the best advice is always to seek out the advice of a qualified PGA professional who is not only up to date with the latest designs on the market, but who can look at your swing and help you to identify the clubs that will best suit your needs as an individual. Trading in the long irons for a couple of lofted fairway woods is something I recommend to all recreational golfers.

In this respect, technology can help you to a better game. It takes skill and a great deal of practice to be proficient with a long iron, so why not carry a 5- and a 7-wood (even a 9-wood) that can help you to hit shots of between 170 and 220 yards with a much greater degree of confidence? In years gone by, a set of 'matched' irons off the shelf included a pitching wedge and sand iron, but such has been the explosion in the choice of specialist wedges of varying lofts and designs that good players in particular nowadays prefer to buy these clubs individually, 'customising' their set according to personal taste.

One swing fits all...

Now that you have learned the nuts and bolts of the grip and the set-up, and have the makings of a sound, repeating swing, the next step is to apply these skills to each of the clubs in the bag – right the way from the driver down to a lofted wedge. And before we go any further, a point I want to make perfectly clear is that *you don't have to learn a different swing to play all of these different shots.* As long as you adhere to the fundamentals listed in the previous chapters, it's simply a matter of understanding the subtle adjustments that need to be made within the address position to accommodate clubs of varying

length and loft – and then trusting your swing to deliver the goods.

There are obvious differences in the length and the lie of the individual clubs, but following the set-up routines I have illustrated in the previous chapters will guarantee a text-book posture in each case, whereupon the 'chain reaction' that we have talked about can take over.

The following 'key-note' images will help you to play four shots that form the basis of a sound long game: (1) driving the ball off the tee, (2) playing a fairway wood for position, (3) approach play with a mid-iron and (4) a full wedge shot from 100 yards or so of the green. The general shape of the swing associated with each of the four shots is illustrated with a mini-sequence, but the most important images are the pull-outs that I have included to convey what I believe to be the most important aspects of technique and 'feel' in each case. Not only will this teach you a little more about the way a good swing gels together, based on the fundamentals of a good set-up, but it will prepare you to follow smart strategy on the course, and attach certain sensations to certain types of shot.

So, on that note, let's head for the tee.

• ON THE TEE •

To focus your mind on your desired landing area in the fairway is the first step to hitting a good tee-shot.

Driving the ball

Golfers the world over share a recurring dream: they want to hit the ball harder, straighter, and farther. Any time I stand in front of a group of golfers and ask which of the 14 clubs any one of them would like to master, the chorus is nearly unanimous: 'The Driver!' I'd stake the house on it.

Be warned, however, that this natural exuberance to want to get out there and hit the ball as far as you can has to be tempered with some realistic forward thinking as far as your strategy is concerned. One of the first problems you will encounter with the driver is that as you walk on to the tee you are often confronted with such a wide expanse of area to aim at that it's easy to become blasé in your alignment. What you must learn to do is narrow your focus, and single out the smallest possible target – say, the edge of a bunker or a point on the horizon, a tree top or such

like. That way you get tuned-in to hitting a specific target. To stand there and aim 'at the fairway' is not a meaningful enough goal. Fall into that trap and your mindset is much too 'loose'. So, rule No.1 is *always study the shape of the hole to get an idea of where best to place the ball off the tee, and then identify a specific target that funnels you towards achieving that goal.*

One final point before we look at the swing itself. When it comes to choosing a driver, I would hesitate using much below 9 degrees of loft. Most amateur players are better off with a minimum of 10 and perhaps even 11 degrees. That extra loft not only gives you greater confidence when you look down on it, but it will reduce sidespin, so you not only get the ball up in the air a lot easier, but you will find that you hit the ball consistently straighter. Again, talk to your professional.

Key-note 1:
Driver set-up creates a 'launch pad'

The speed that you generate at impact determines how far you hit the ball, so the focus with a driver has to be on maximizing your clubhead speed *without* sacrificing accuracy, and thus plant that speed squarely on the back of the ball. To do that you have to think in terms of catching the ball fractionally on the upswing – and that requires you to play the ball forward in your stance, opposite the inside of the left heel, where it waits to be 'collected' as the clubhead begins its ascent.

This sweeping action through impact is what enables good drivers of the ball to flight these shots with a trajectory that maximizes overall distance off the tee (a combination of carry through the air and run on the fairway). A descending angle produces a weak hit and too much spin – a tell tale sign is if you have ball marks on top of your driver.

Following this routine will help you to get into the habit of adopting a consistent set-up with the driver. Start with your feet close together, and measure off the ball position in relation to your left heel before moving the right foot away from the left to establish the width of your stance. In the final analysis, your hands should be fractionally behind the ball, while your left arm and the clubshaft should be seen to form a comfortable straight line. You are now ideally positioned to turn and shift your weight and *collect* the ball with a powerful sweeping motion. A light grip pressure completes the picture, leaving the hands and arms relaxed, promoting both rhythm and speed.

These adjustments to the set-up make perfect sense when you stop and think about what you are actually trying to achieve. We're talking about the

Measure off the ball position in relation to your left heel, then adjust the width of the stance with the right foot.

longest club in the bag, and as such it requires that you first of all establish a sound base. There's a balance to be struck between *stability* and *mobility*, but you will find that you achieve the ideal combination if

you spread your feet to the full width of your shoulders, and turn your toes on both feet out a little. Stand tall and make the most of your height before you gently flex your knees for balance. You want to feel that your weight is settled 60:40 in favour of your right side, and you should also be aware of the fact that your spine angle is now tilted away from the target, placing your head slightly behind the ball.

One more thing. The sweet-spot on these modern drivers is actually quite high up the clubface, so it's important that you tee the ball up fairly high. Most amateur players tend to tee the ball too low, which contributes to hitting *down* on it too steeply. To avoid that trap, make sure that at least half the ball is visible above the top of the clubface. This further invites you to hit 'up' on the ball through impact.

Reminder! Exaggerate the feeling...

A great way to get a sense of the 'launch-pad' feeling you are looking for at the set-up with a driver is to rehearse your routine on an upslope. Doing this naturally settles the majority of your weight on your right side, and at the same time encourages you to angle your spine away from the target, which is exactly the look you want to create. Flex your knees and feel the athletic pressure in your right thigh, ready to absorb the turn of the upper body as you wind up your backswing and truly get behind the ball. Rehearse this action for a couple of minutes, then take those feelings with you on to the tee.

Swing cue: Start low, and create width

Once you are comfortable over the ball, start your swing with a 'low-and-slow' move that promises your upper body all the time it needs to complete a full 'wind-up'. This unhurried move at the start of the swing gets the coiling process underway. Make it a smooth 'one-piece' action, the arms and shoulders maintaining their relationship with the clubhead as it moves away on the desired inside track.

To think 'low and slow' has the further benefit that it involves the whole of the body in starting the swing, which immediately eliminates some of the problems associated with picking the club up too quickly with the hands and losing the natural radius. *What you are trying to create here is a wonderful circu-* *lar motion with the clubhead, and the better your rhythm, the more speed you will enjoy as you accelerate into the ball.* Swing at a comfortable pace and you simply give yourself a better chance of winding and unwinding your body in sequence, the long term benefit being that you are then on track to create a shallow 'flat spot' at the bottom of the swing (again, perfect for sweeping the ball away).

Many great players (Jack Nicklaus and Nick Faldo among them) have found that hovering the clubhead at address helps to promote this wide move away from the ball. Grounding the clubhead at address can sometimes lead to a jerky first move, but if you hover the clubhead a little off the ground you do tend to find that the club glides away from the ball, and that sets you on the way to a full backswing. Give it a try.

Imagine creating a wide circular motion and you will get your swing off to the perfect start.

Swing cue:
Turn and 'stretch' to the top

As a result of your good work at the set-up, and in getting started smoothly, the top of your backswing should see the bigger muscles in your upper body fully coiled against the resistance of a stable lower body action. Think of the legs as the shock-absorbers that counter the powerful turning of the upper body. Focus on the right knee: maintain the flex you created at address and feel yourself turning against it. That will reward you with a real sense of 'coil' and elasticity as you reach the top.

My view here is that the 'sequencing' of the swing is the key to a consistent and powerful position at the top. While the hands and arms appear to initiate the early movement of the clubhead away from the ball (and basically get the chain reaction started smoothly), it's the upper body which then takes over to complete the backswing movement. One thing I notice with good players is that at about halfway back the shoulders have not fully turned. Many amateurs have a full turn at this stage then simply lift to the top. The correct sequence is the triangle of arms and shoulders moves away the wrists hinge to get the club swinging up on a good plane, and then the upper body completes its turn. This is the key to winding up the backswing and coiling the body. The upper body winds over the lower half, and the benefit of this athletic and well-coordinated action is that it creates the energy (the 'recoil') that drives the downswing.

As you work on gearing your own swing, try to picture in your mind the turning motion of the body and the swinging of the arms and the club being completed at pretty much the same time as you reach the top. In reality there will be a slight 'lag' (a result of the logical 'gearing' as the hips stop turning before the shoulders, while the arms and hands travel that bit further in response to the weight and momentum of the swinging clubhead). But having

that image of the arms and body completing the backswing together will go a long way towards their matching up on the way down. And that's the secret to solid and consistent ball-striking.

Braced right knee and thigh resist the coiling action and stabilize the swing generally.

Driver drill:
Turn behind it...and stay behind it

Driving the ball solidly demands that you wind and unwind your body efficiently to maximize the centrifugal force that accelerates the arms, hands and (ultimately) the clubhead. In other words, you have to do everything in your power to maximize your 'coil'. With the driver, you want to be aware of the right knee acting as a brace, *resisting* the turning of the hips and upper body. This drill will help you. Adopt a good posture, standing your driver in front of you to approximate the ball position, and steady it with your left hand. Then rehearse the movement of the swing, making a wide sweeping motion with the right hand as you turn the entire right side of your body away to create the backswing move. Sense that your weight is shifting onto your right side as you turn against that braced right knee and thigh. Let your head ease gently to the right to assist you in turning your shoulders, to the point you get your back to the target and your left shoulder under the chin.

From here, as you go on to unwind and accelerate into the downswing, you want to feel that your upper body and your head remains steady behind the ball as you release the right arm to return the hand squarely to impact. Working on this exercise between hitting shots will develop the powerful action you need to release the clubhead more forcefully and sweep the ball off the tee.

Use this exercise to get the feeling of turning your upper body behind the ball, and then releasing that energy with an upward sweeping motion.

Turn your back on the target as you coil your body and 'load' up your swing.

Head and upper body stay behind the ball as you unwind and accelerate into impact.

Swing cue: Maximize speed, maximize distance

Having made that backswing coil, and created all that energy, the most important thing now is that you retain it as you change direction. And again, it's the sequence of events that determines your fate. It works like this. As you complete your backswing coil you create and store an energy

that is about to be unlocked as you change direction. For a split second, your body is actually moving in two directions at once; just as you arrive at the top, so you are at the same time starting your motion forwards. The left knee moves towards the target, and then the hips and trunk begin to unwind as your weight shifts back to the left side. In doing this you will find that your arms drop the club into this wonderful hitting position. And this is your green light to accelerate hard, the right knee, right hip, right arm and right shoulder firing on all cylinders as you release the club and collect the ball cleanly off the tee.

When you ask good players what they do to hit the ball further, most will say that they try to swing the club more slowly and deliberately. What they mean is they make an effort to make the transition as smooth as possible in order to maximize the recoil and acceleration. This is the element of 'timing' that is so important: Have the patience to build your speed gradually, and the swinging motion of the arms will 'match up' with the rotary motion of your body coming into the ball, and that's the recipe for solid impact.

Swing easy, hit hard – the key to maximizing your speed and acceleration (and distance!) is to unwind smoothly from the top of the backswing.

Final frame: Free-wheel to a 'wrap-around' finish

One of the best swing thoughts to have with the driver is that you maximize your shoulder turn – both on the way back and on the way through. Certainly, I see too many golfers who fail to complete their swing in either direction. A simple cue is to turn the left shoulder under the chin on the backswing, and the right shoulder under the chin on the follow through. Make this your chief swing thought with the driver and you will reap the benefit of a full coiling action of the upper body on the backswing, a better weight transfer and a more powerful release. And as a result of the speed you have built up you will enjoy free-wheeling all the way to a full finish, your energy totally spent.

That's the sensation you must go after with the driver. This is the longest and most powerful swing you make, so make a real 'swish' with the clubhead through impact, and enjoy the feeling of a full 'wrap-around' finish, chest facing the target, and your weight fully supported on the left side.

Practise turning, swishing and posing at the finish!

• 170 YARDS + •

Playing for distance & position

I always feel the acid test of a good swing is the quality of the strike and the trajectory of the shot with the long irons – the 2-, 3- and 4-irons. If a player is hitting those clubs well, he or she can be pretty confident they have a good action going. The long irons are tough to hit because they require that you generate a significant amount of clubhead speed in order to produce a good trajectory, which is why most amateur golfers are better off leaving these clubs well alone, and opting instead for a 5- and 7-wood.

In fact, if you are upwards of a 90s shooter, I would go as far to suggest that you discard anything longer than a 4-iron, and carry a 5-, a 7- and even a 9-wood as replacements. Having a lower centre of gravity, and a wide sole, these clubs are far more forgiving, and will help you to get the ball into the air. When you have a club with a relatively wide face to it, you don't have to

swing perfectly to hit it well, and so you're not under pressure to generate that much speed. A lofted wood is also more likely to give you a higher trajectory shot which will land the ball more softly on the green. So, all things considered, a much friendlier option.

Lofted fairway woods are also perfect for those 'lay-up' shots on the longer holes. Imagine a typical situation, the sort you might find at any long par four or par five hole. The green is all but out of reach, and to attempt to shoot straight at it is simply inviting trouble. There are times when the risk might be worthwhile – say, in matchplay, when all you stand to lose is one hole. But if you had a card in your hand, the only smart shot is a positional one. This is where good course management skills take over, the key being to consult your yardage chart and identify a safe landing area, leaving you a with the chance of getting down with a pitch and a putt. Nine times out of ten, a smooth swing with a utility wood is the answer.

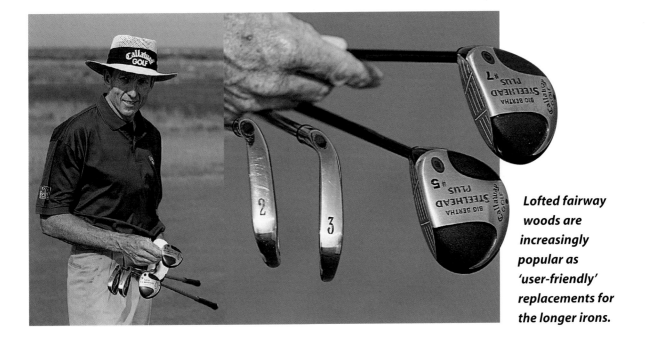

Lofted fairway woods are increasingly popular as 'user-friendly' replacements for the longer irons.

Swing cue:
Prime your swing at the set-up

The set-up and the general shape of the swing with a long iron or fairway wood varies little to that employed with the driver. This is a slightly shorter-shafted club, and the feet are fractionally closer together at the set-up because of that. But this is still a fairly substantial stance, and one that provides the stability for what is going to be a fairly full turn of the upper body. The weight distribution is perhaps now a little more even between the feet, while the ball is forward in the stance, placed about an inch inside the left heel.

The key difference between this and the driver swing is as much a visual one as anything else, in that I'm now looking for a 'level' release (as opposed to that slight upward sweeping motion). That's the key to this shot, and as a cue, it's worth rehearsing this action before you make your swing. Give your senses a preview of what you are aiming to achieve both at impact and immediately through the ball; extend your arms and *ease* the club forwards into the follow-through, maintaining all the width that you are looking for as the clubhead travels through impact.

A small, lofted fairway wood looks inviting behind the ball, and that's great for your confidence.

When you swing for real, think in terms of 'chasing' the clubhead after the ball as you unwind towards the target. This will promote the shallow swing that you need to strike these shots with real authority. The sensation is of 'brushing' the turf through impact – you basically catch the ball and the turf at the same time.

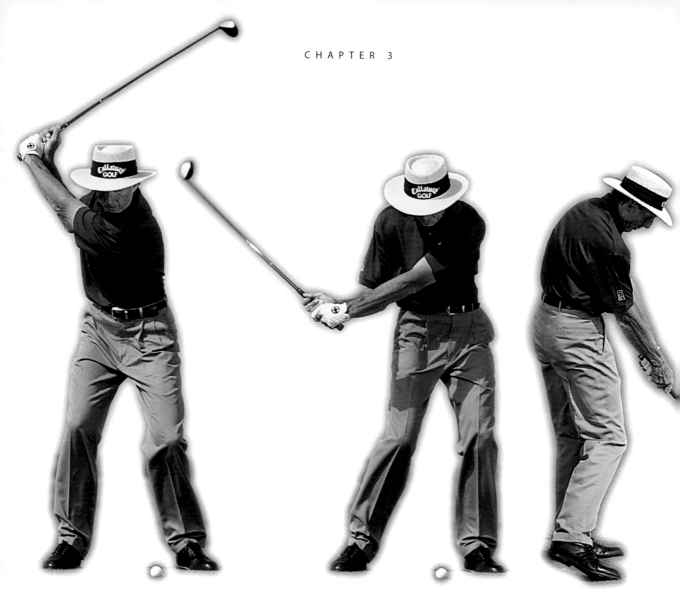

Swing cue: Swing through impact (not to it)

One of the reasons amateurs have trouble hitting long irons (and fairway woods!), clubs which have relatively little loft on the face, is that they get anxious and want to 'lift' the ball into the air. Often associated with this is a tendency to straighten the legs through impact as they 'flip' at the ball with the hands. To get over that problem you have to get this visual image of sweeping the ball and brushing the turf fixed in your mind, and then commit yourself 100% to the shot.

Your job is to create what I describe as a 'level'

swing through impact, one that delivers the natural loft on the clubface as you sweep the ball off the turf. Good players release the club with a free-wheeling extension through the ball, and the forces at work pull the arms and the club towards the target. This holds true whether you are playing a driver, a fairway wood, a mid-iron or a wedge, but it is particularly important with the longer clubs.

One of the dangers when learning golf is that we speak of the impact position as being all-important,

Commit yourself to the shot and trust the club to do its job as you swing all the way through impact.

and tend to forget that the swing still has some way to go. Let me stress here that impact is a position you swing *through*. You have to rotate your body all the way to the finish. The moment you get anxious, or think about hitting at the ball with the hands, the shot is over. You create the situation where the clubhead is decelerating through impact, and the ball never has a chance to get into the air. But as soon as you commit yourself to turning your body all the way through the shot you will release the club freely.

Make that your primary swing thought as you step up to the ball. Once you have completed the backswing, wait for your moment, and let the club-head effortlessly 'collect' the ball as you turn your body all the way through to a balanced finish. Do it right and you will experience a wonderful sensation as the clubhead strikes the ball sweetly and clips the turf – the solid feeling up the shaft into your hands and the knowledge that the ball is on its way towards your intended target. A job well done.

• APPROACH PLAY •

170 yards and in: Entering the 'strike' zone

Good iron players swing the club at a speed they can comfortably control, and never force the ball with a mid- to short iron. Within striking distance of the pin, the emphasis must be on striking the ball solidly to create the backspin that flights the ball with a controlled trajectory and lands it softly on the green. Ideally, with anything from, say, a 5-iron down, you are looking for a crisp ball-turf contact that promises accurate shot-making, a shallow divot pattern, and consistent distance control. In short, any time you are firing at the green, accuracy is the only real issue that should concern you. And the key quality here is *rhythm*.

Watch most tour players and you will find they hit these shots with a compact, almost three-quarter action. They swing *within* themselves, and that's a lesson you will do well to pick up on. The trouble is that ego and expectation tend to get in the way of realistic club selection. Just because you once hit a 7-iron 160 yards, don't think you will do it

every time. You have to be more realistic. As you study the shot, gauge your yardage and think about where you want to land the ball on the green. *Don't flirt with hazards, but keep to the safe side. And always take enough club that you reach pin high.* This is a controlled shot. Swing too hard with the more lofted irons and you put more spin on the ball, causing it to spiral into the air, which makes judgement of distance a lottery. The irons are *direction* clubs, not distance clubs, and I guarantee that you will improve your ball-striking overnight if you simply focus on playing these shots with a shorter and more compact action.

To achieve that, keep the feet flat on the ground as much as possible as a direct means of restricting your hip turn, which will basically tighten up the coil in the backswing and give you a much more consistent position at the top. That will give you a real sense of stability in the lower body providing the base for a good upper body turn and a controlled arm swing.

Ball-then-turf: a shallow divot pattern is one of the vital signs of crisp iron play.

Look for this compact, three-quarter action. That's all you need to control both the flight and the landing distance of your iron shots.

Once again the set-up reflects the type of shot that you are intending to play. As far as the width and stance and ball position go, you may have noticed a sort of sliding scale in operation, the width of the stance narrowing (albeit fractionally) with each step down, and the ball creeping further back. As a rough guide, I'd suggest that when you're using anything from a 5- to an 8-iron you play the ball just forward of the middle of the stance, where the clubhead can meet it as it is approaching the bottom of the arc. This

feature of the set-up gives you a look where the club-shaft is angled nicely towards the target, the hands comfortably ahead of the ball (see pages 94–95).

(Note that these are not hard and fast rules, and it's up to you to go out and experiment. Depending on the exact nature of your swing, adjusting the position an inch or so either way can make a big difference to the way that you strike the ball.)

I should stress also that as you set-up to a mid- to short iron, your body always takes its orders from the

position of the clubface. Get that leading edge aimed dead on your target before you settle into your posture. From then on, your job is to create that controlled swing that promises solid contact. I mentioned a moment ago that a good key is to keep your feet grounded, as that helps to minimize weight transfer and lower body motion generally. The upper body turns about the natural axis of the spine, and the arm-swing is timed to match. Look for the hands to swing to about 11 o'clock on the backswing through to 1 o'clock on the way through. That's all you need to play controlled iron shots. Those of you who like to check other details should look for the wrists to be nicely hinged and the clubface to be in a 'neutral' position as you reach the top (i.e. angled at about 45 degrees, the clubface matching the back of the left hand).

Repeat business: though the club may change according to the distance you have to land the ball, the shape and the rhythm of your swing should not.

Here we have the 7-iron sequence face on, and from this angle the compact nature of the swing is clearly evident. Placing the ball towards the middle of the stance helps to ensure a crisp downward blow which is what you are looking for with the mid- to short irons.

• STRATEGY •

For greater consistency, play to the count of four...

Another thing that will certainly help you to a more consistent performance with the mid to short irons is *routine*. It's all a matter of standardizing your actions, and a disciplined routine actually takes away much of the indecision that can get in the way of striking these shots solidly. One way to improve this aspect of your iron play is to think about playing to the count of 'four'. Having sized up the shot and made your club selection, count yourself in: On the count of 'one' you look at your target to get a good image of the shot; 'two', you look back at the ball; 'three' is the cue to make your backswing, and 'four' is the downswing that hits the ball.

Focusing on this procedure gets your mind and body tuned in to following simple orders, and takes away the confusion that may otherwise surround the shot you are about to play. All that is replaced with: TARGET...BALL...SWING...HIT. Keep it simple, and you automatically keep your swing ticking over.

I mentioned earlier the benefit of playing these shots with a fairly compact action, and it is certainly my belief that keeping the feet flat on the ground throughout the backswing is an effective thought in producing a controlled, three-quarter length swing – one that repeats.

• THE FULL WEDGE •

All about air traffic control

From 100 yards or so of the flag your aim is to get the ball as close to the hole as possible, and at the very worst hit the green. And let me stress up front that these shots are all about *accuracy*, not distance. Governed more or less by the arms and upper body, this is not a full swing and does not involve the body in a forceful way. From inside wedge range, the emphasis is on controlling the trajectory of your shots and landing the ball a specific distance. To do that, the consistency of your rhythm has to be uppermost in your mind. If you feel you are struggling to reach a certain distance with a wedge, take a nine. That's about as complicated as strategy gets from this critical scoring distance. Be realistic in your assessment of every shot, always take the extra club if necessary, and swing comfortably within your ability.

Set-up cue:
Get ready for impact

One of the fundamentals emphasized throughout this book is that the set-up position pre-determines the nature of impact. The way you stand in relation to the ball reflects your intentions on that particular shot in terms of the strike that you are hoping to achieve. Looking face-on, the set-up for this full wedge shot is remarkable only for the fact that my stance is now fairly narrow, weight fairly evenly spread, and the ball positioned more or less in the middle of the feet. We are using the shortest and most lofted irons in the bag, and the set-up has simply been pre-shrunk to fit the playing characteristics of the club.

It's the view down the line that reveals the most significant adjustment you have to make in preparation to play these shots to the green, in that the feet are now slightly open in relation to the target line (while the hips and shoulders remain square). This subtle adjustment not only gives you a good feel for this length of shot, but a slightly open stance serves to restrict the amount of turn on the backswing that you have in the lower body. And that's key in terms of your consistency from this range. This is a swing that is governed by the rotary motion

of the upper body, the arms and shoulders controlling the club with what is a compact three-quarter swing. There is no real weight shift to speak of, and so you don't want the hips or the lower body to get too involved. A great swing thought on these

shots is to keep the lower body 'quiet'. Remember, this shot is all about accuracy, not distance, and while the body is important in terms of providing a consistent framework to the swing, it is not really called upon to generate speed.

Swing drill: Right arm creates the width

your right hip. Then, with the right hand only, swing the club to this three-quarter backswing position. Feel the weight of the clubhead on the end of the shaft and let the club create its own natural radius as you swing the right arm freely and easily into position. Don't make the mistake of hugging the right elbow in tight to the side your body, but give it the freedom to work out and up to this comfortable position. Placing and keeping the left hand on the left hip as you rehearse the backswing further reminds you to keep the hips quiet as you turn the upper body, and when you then reunite your left hand with the right, you find yourself in the perfect backswing position. A compact, three-quarter swing with all the width you need to strike the ball crisply towards the target. All you have to do then is repeat the sensation when you play the shot for real.

Creating width is one of the keys to striking short irons with confidence, and the exercise you see here provides a very easy reminder whenever you are practising or preparing to play a shot out on the course. (It also rein-forces the importance of making a compact three-quarter swing, which I believe to be one of the golden rules for consistent short iron play.)

It works like this. Adopt your regular set-up, but then take your left hand off the grip and place it on

The swing:
Arms and body in perfect harmony

Adopting that slightly open stance is all part of this concept of 'pre-setting' the impact position at address, which really is one of the secrets for this shot. In the case of a short iron, it promotes the synchronised arm and body motion that you're looking for to make a repeating swing. A compact, three-quarter action further enhances your overall sense of balance and accuracy – vital ingredients whenever you are within sight of the pin.

Within this atmosphere, all else goes on as normal. The wrists hinge to get the club swinging up on a good plane, and as you then unwind you enjoy a wonderful sense of hitting down and through the ball as the hands release to deliver the natural loft on the clubface. The upper body is the engine that drives the arms and hands along, and focusing your eyes on the back of the ball keeps you turning about a steady axis. You are using the most lofted and upright clubs

in the bag, and as a result your swing is naturally going to be fairly steep into the ball, and this enables you to produce considerable backspin. That's a natural consequence of good wedge technique. The shorter shaft also helps to reduce the length of your swing, which is a good thing in terms of control. To further enhance that control you may want to experiment gripping (or 'choking') down the club, especially as the target gets closer.

The greatest danger on these lofted approach shots is decelerating the club through impact. So as you visualize the shot, remind yourself to be positive, and accelerate all the way through the ball to a balanced finish. Feel the weight of the clubhead and *swing* it. The confident release of the right hand (and right side generally) is one of the keys to pure ball-striking, and as you improve your technique you will find that you can actually accelerate hard through impact and yet still produce shots that seem to float softly towards the target. And the better your action through the ball, the more accurate you will be.

CHAPTER 4

Round and about the cup

**IN THE LONG TERM,
THE SHORT-GAME IS KING**

To cut your scores from the high 90s to the low-80s is going to take a certain amount of work in terms of improving the shape of your swing and the general quality of your ball-striking. It's a process of rationalization; above all else, you have to eliminate the destructive shots that lead to big numbers – the double and triple-bogeys. And worse. The first rule to shooting lower scores is *keep the ball in play*. Most mid-teen handicappers play perhaps a dozen good holes and then 'blow-out'. Working towards healthier basics that reward you with a more consistent swing is no guarantee of hitting great shots, but what it will do is make your 'misses' that

much better. If you can get around 18 holes with no worse than bogey on the card, you're well on the way to shooting good scores.

The bottom line is that to capitalize on improvements in your ball striking you have to work on the short-game skills. The reason average club handicaps remain stuck at around the 20 mark is that golfers simply don't spend enough time working on their skills inside wedge range. And yet this is where golf gets serious. Mathematics has never been my strong point, but the figures do seem compelling: *Putting accounts for almost 50% of the shots you hit during the course of a round, and when you add to the mix all of the*

chipping, pitching and greenside bunker shots, you're looking at probably 80% of the game. These skills are simply too important to be ignored. In fact, the next time you play, add up how many times you take more than 2 shots to get into the hole from within, say, 50 yards of the green – this then is potentially how many shots you can cut off your score with a decent short game.

In other aspects of the game physical limitations may prevent you achieving certain goals. But there is nothing about the short game that requires exceptional strength or a spectacular degree of coordination. Time, yes. You do have to be prepared to put in some practice. But with a little effort, these are the skills that everybody who plays golf ought to be able to get to grips with…and have fun improving.

To illustrate the simplicity of what I refer to as a 'family short-game', I am going to start on the green with a look at what makes a good putting stroke tick, and work back from there into the realm of chipping, pitching and sand play. We saw in the full swing that good technique involved synchronizing a good body action with a compact arm swing, and that's exactly what we're looking for here – the only difference being that these are not power shots, so there's less emphasis on turning your body to create clubhead speed, and more on synchronizing the hands, arms

and upper body to control a simple motion. In all of the following skills, the real fun lies in 'playing the detective'. The more you experience different situations and playing conditions, the better prepared you will be to make the right decision and play the appropriate shot. And nowhere is the room for thoughtful experimentation more profitable.

All about putting

It seems to me that the greatest putters in the game are those that learn to aim the putter correctly. This may sound like a rather obvious statement to make, but the fact is that many golfers (and even good ones) aim and set-up poorly. And unless you can get the putter aimed correctly along your chosen line to the hole, and back it up with a posture that allows you to create a repeating stroke that returns the putter-face squarely to the ball at impact, you're going to be fighting a losing battle.

The danger then is that what on the face of it is a straightforward matter becomes a mental problem. More than any other part of the game, putting has the ability to turn the mind against you very quickly. You can avoid much of that confusion by following common rules – the first of which is always lay some clubs down to check your alignment.

• THE BASICS •

The basics:
Simple advice for perfect alignment

Most good golfers work on the principle of creating a simple pendulum motion with the putter, a concept which both demands and revolves around a good set up position. There is some individuality in the way that people take their grip and their stance, and so on, but there are obvious common denominators to a good method: *the putter face must be travelling square to the line at the moment of impact* being the most important. People achieve this in different ways, but the crux of the matter is that the putter-face is square at impact. Develop a stroke that delivers you that, and it's then a case of honing your feel for distance.

Setting up to a putt, the key is to get yourself comfortable, and in a position that sees the feet, hips and shoulders 'square', parallel to the ball-to-target line. To get a good perspective of the putt, you want to bend from the hips until your eye-line is over (or just slightly inside) the ball. You can check this easily by 'plumbing' a club from the bridge of your nose. Bring the palms of your hands together and you establish a comfortable posture. Your body is now said to be 'square' and your head is angled correctly, your eyes perfectly placed to focus on the line to the hole.

The basics: Feel the 'connection'

One of the words I tend to use a lot in my teaching is 'linkage'. Both in the full swing and the short game, this refers to the close nature of the relationship between the arms and the chest. A fault a lot of people make when they set up to a putt is that they splay their elbows out, which causes the arms to wander all over the place in the stroke itself. To correct this, take a moment to check that as you allow your arms to hang from the shoulders, the elbows turn inwards, palms showing. Then, when you turn your palms to

'Linking' the arms with the upper body promotes a repeating stroke.

face one another, you will find that your arms and upper body are nicely 'linked up'. As a result, your stroke will be connected to the movement of your chest – and more reliable for that.

When you focus on achieving this linkage at the set-up, you will also find that your hands assume a better position under the chin. Ideally, with the putter sitting squarely behind the ball, you want to create this slightly arched look in the left wrist. That will further help to keep the arms (and the putter shaft) working in a near vertical plane, which helps you to produce a solid repeating stroke.

Create a putting 'corridor', and groove your action from inside 10 feet.

Arms and shoulders create a simple pendulum motion, and the putter runs back and forth on a natural path.

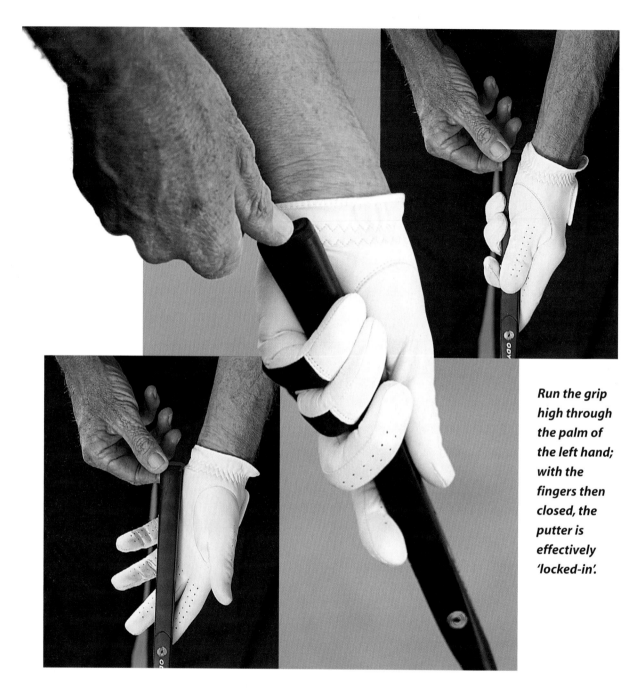

Run the grip high through the palm of the left hand; with the fingers then closed, the putter is effectively 'locked-in'.

The basics: Left-hand grip is a 'lock'

There are few things worse for your full swing than, when gripping the club, having it run too high through the palm of the left hand. An accentuated palm grip threatens the mobility in the left wrist, and that costs you speed and distance. But with a putter in your hands, you want to promote minimal wrist action, so holding it up high against the fleshy pad at the base of the left thumb can actually help you to keep your wrists passive throughout the stroke. With a 'palm grip', the putter feels locked in.

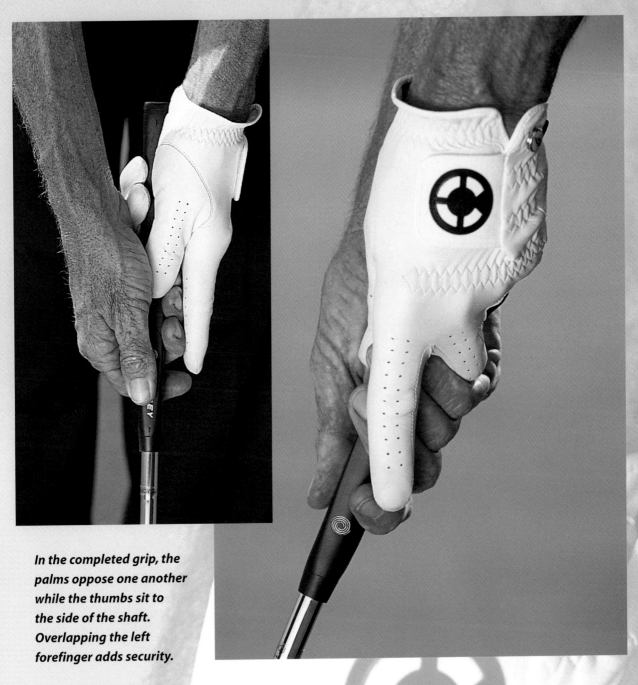

In the completed grip, the palms oppose one another while the thumbs sit to the side of the shaft. Overlapping the left forefinger adds security.

To further reinforce the security of the left wrist, many golfers favour what's known as the 'reverse-overlap' style of grip, which sees the left forefinger draped over the fingers on the right hand. In the stroke itself, this gives you a great sense of the left hand guiding the putter-head through the ball.

The basics:
Understand the path of the stroke

I hope that by now you are well versed in the notion that to make a sound putting stroke your arms and upper body must work 'together'. The overall motion is controlled by the gentle rocking of the shoulders to create the pendulum-like movement that swings the putter back and through on a natural, repeating path. The distance between the elbows is maintained throughout the stroke – in fact, the triangle between the arms and the shoulders is consistent from start to finish. It's really a matter of rocking the shoulders and allowing the arms and hands to respond naturally, without any independent movement of the hands. Providing a vital balance and calm posture, the lower body is 'quiet' and perfectly balanced throughout.

To get an idea of the way the putter head tracks back and forth, put a couple of clubs down on the green to form a corridor when you practise. On short putts (say, up to 15 feet or so), the putter-head moves pretty well straight-back and straight-through. But as the putt gets longer, the clubhead will follow the path of a regular swing – i.e. it moves slightly inside the ball-to-target line, both back and through. That's basic geometry at work, and once you have the makings of a stroke like this, it's then a case of practising different length putts to develop your sense of 'feel' – the ability to roll the ball a desired distance.

• DRILLS TO PEP-UP YOUR PRACTICE •

A practice putting session should involve a few minutes first of all working on basic technique, reflecting on the fundamentals of alignment and posture, as discussed, and repeating a concise stroke to hole putts from inside 10 feet. After that, I recommend you turn your attention to pace, and focus on certain exercises that keep you in touch with the speed of the greens so that you perfect this ability to 'lag' the ball close to the hole from all corners of the green.

Here are just a few ideas to get you started. Whatever your ability, any time you can spend on the putting green will reward you out on the course. It's amazing what a few holed putts can do for your confidence – not just on the greens, but for your game in general.

How to keep the putter running on track

As long as you maintain that link between the upper part of your arms and your chest, gently rocking the shoulders will give you a very solid-looking stroke. The feel you are looking for here is that the left shoulder works down on the backswing and then up on the through-swing; this will keep the putter moving back and forth on a natural path. You can easily check the line of your stroke by running the putter-head back and forth along the shaft of a club on the ground (or the flagstick while you are waiting for your turn to putt on the course). Keep it in mind that the length of your stroke will determine the speed at which the ball is released, but also that good putters aim to *accelerate* the putter-head through the ball and execute their stroke with a repeating rhythm. To ensure you do the same, focus on making your follow-through slightly longer than the backswing.

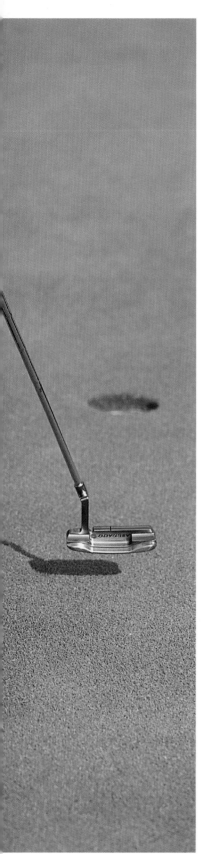

'Brush' it into the hole

Find a straight putt of four feet or so, and get yourself set up to make your regular stroke. Then, without the benefit of a backswing, push and brush the ball into the back of the hole and check to see that the putter-face finishes square to the line. You want to feel that your arms and shoulders work as a unit as they provide the motion and gently accelerate the putter-head through on that line. Think in terms of the back of the left hand being the putter face, and it finishing square to the line.

I find this exercise is particularly beneficial to players who may be susceptible to collapsing the left wrist through impact. Do this for a couple of minutes, then go after the same brushing sensation as you hit short putts with your regular stroke.

Another good practice tip that you might try in conjunction with this drill is to slip a pen into your glove, down the back of the left hand, and keep it there as you hit putts. That will give you a terrific sensation of keeping the left wrist secure through the stroke, the two hands working together as a secure guiding unit as you create that pendulum action. What this does is basically reinforce that security in the left wrist. Remember, the hands, arms and shoulders work as a guiding until to create a repeating stroke – any independent action in the wrists and the mechanism breaks down.

Permanent fix: stick a marker pen down the back of your glove and enjoy the sensation of keeping the left wrist firm as you stroke the ball into the back of the hole.

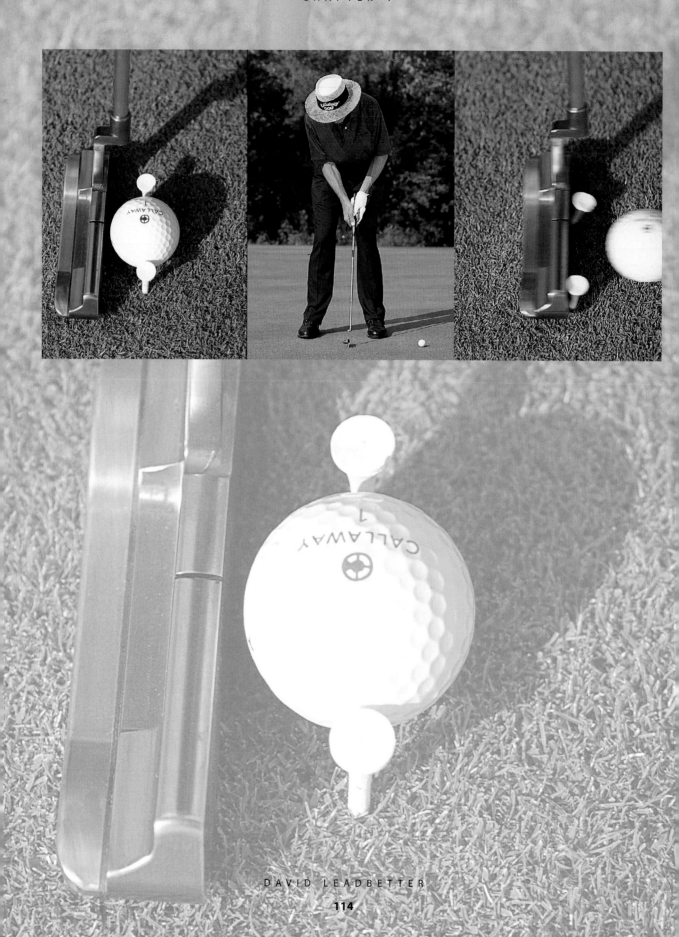

'Trap the gate' for a positive roll

Having the ball come solidly off the middle of the putter-face is the key to starting the ball on line and rolling it consistently on the green. Mis-hit the ball, without that positive acceleration, and you're in trouble. The drill you see here can help you to train your stroke and result in you making solid contact more often.

All you have to do is stick two tees into the green to make a small gate, one that's just wide enough for the ball to fit through. Place a ball in the gate so that only half of it is there to be struck, and then make your stroke, rapping the putter against the gate to set the ball running towards the back of the hole. Focus on trapping the ball and the tees together, so that the putter-face strikes the gate flush every time. In just a few minutes, this will give you a terrific sense of striking your putts with real authority – as you should from this range.

Another benefit of this drill is that it teaches you the importance of keeping your head nice and still over the ball. The trick is to keep your eyes focused on the tees (as opposed to following the ball) as you make your stroke and hold your finish. Do that and you will find that you keep your head and your body steady all the way through impact – another important factor in the search for a consistent stroke.

Improve your rhythm, and ROLL the ball

I advise working on a relatively short, compact action from close range. But as you get further out, so your stroke will get longer and move progressively inside the ball-to-target line. That's perfectly natural. Just make sure that as the length of the putt increases, your rhythm remains consistent. Think in terms of saying to yourself, 'one' as you flow the putter back and 'two' as you then release it on the way through. A light grip pressure will enable you to do this

instinctively. One thing you must never do, particularly on a lengthy putt, is make a short backswing and then stab at the ball in the mistaken belief you can determine the weight of the putt at the moment of impact. The only safe way to control the distance you roll the ball is to 'measure' the length of your stroke, increasing it as required to create more momentum and speed off the putter.

Hitting a few putts with the right hand is a great way to improve this 'feel' and get a sense of releasing the putter to get the ball rolling across the green. What I particularly like about this drill is the way it highlights this element of 'lag' in the hand as the wrist 'gives' in to the weight of the putter. It's one of those intangible qualities that can be hard to understand until you experience it yourself. So swing the putter with the right hand only, and get the ball *rolling*.

Work on touch and distance control

Long putts are all about judging the pace at which you roll the ball on the green. What you need is a smooth, *flowing* stroke. Think about bowling a ball – you would make a long, languid motion with your bowling arm and give the ball a good roll. Try to keep that image in mind on approach putting. I think it's a good idea to stand up a little taller when you face a long putt, as that gives you the room to make a longer stroke and create that flowing motion. Then it's all about tuning your sense in to the speed.

Some people believe you should dead roll the ball into the hole, which is okay if the greens are lightning quick and you have a perfect surface. Otherwise I think the ideal pace is that which would see the ball run perhaps 18 inches by the hole should it miss, hence this drill. When you lay a club down about a foot or so beyond the hole that you're putting at, you are reminded to put a positive roll on the ball so that it holds its line. Alternate between your regular grip and right-hand only. Another way to fine-tune your control is to stick a tee in the green and try to 'cluster' three or four balls around it from 20 feet or so. That's a great way to round off your practice session before a game.

For rhythm, 'measure' off your stroke

Watch good putters at work and you will appreciate the way in which they flow the putter through the ball. They swing the putter head with a great sense of rhythm, and this is key in rolling the ball at the desired pace and to the desired distance across the green. To engender this same sense of feel and motion in your own stroke, work on making your follow through at least as long as your backswing. Remember, the only safe way to gauge distance is to measure the length of your stroke to marry up with the length of the putt. In other words, the longer the putt, the longer the stroke, and vice versa.

When you practise, every now and then, you can remind yourself of this by simply laying out a line of balls at regular intervals, as I have done, and measuring your stroke against them as you hit different length putts. Make sure that you swing the putter head the same distance through the ball as you swing it back. I guarantee that after a few minutes your sense of feel will be much improved and you will feel confident in your ability to roll the ball the desired distance to the hole.

Rhythm in equal measure: flow the putter back and through.

• CHIPPING •

*C*hipping, in my book, is a shot played from just off the edge of the green that typically rolls further along the ground than it travels in the air. It's a shot that can be played with just about every club in the bag (professionals these days are even using a fairway wood in certain situations), but as you start out I would suggest you work the scale from a 5- or 6-iron down to a sand iron, your choice of club depending on the ratio of air-to-ground time that is required. What generally happens is that you settle on a couple of favourite clubs for chipping – say a 7-iron for longer chips and a nine for the shorter ones.

Therein lie the real skills you have to acquire to master these shots around the green. The art of *visualisation* and reading the route to the hole is at least as important as the technique involved in play-ing them. Like solving a puzzle, there's a certain satisfaction to be had when you take the right club and land the ball on the perfect spot and watch it turn out just as you planned it. The most important thing when you get around the green is to picture in your mind the shot you want to play (and that applies whether pitching, chipping or playing from sand). The short game is all about a vivid imagination. It's no good walking up to the ball, picking out whatever club you first lay your hands on, and hitting the shot without thinking about what you want to do with the ball. Do your homework, and get a clear image in your head of the perfect shot unfolding before your eyes.

• Leadbetter •
CHIPPING PRACTICE

Here's an exercise I highly recommend. Take a few balls, and work your way around the practice green tossing each one underarm to get an idea of the trajectory and the speed that you're looking for to get close to the hole. Cup the ball in the palm of your hand and release it with the free-flowing motion of the arm. This will give you a terrific understanding of the relationship between flight and roll, which you can then apply to your chipping practice.

The 'chip-putt' – a simple answer to a common problem

One of the reasons I like to have my students work on what I term the 'family' short game is that they can experience how closely related these around-the-green skills are. From the putting stroke, it's just a short hop to a good chipping action. And by way of making that transition, the 'chip-putt' is the perfect solution whenever you find yourself caught in two minds just off the edge of the green. Should you chip it, or should you putt it? If the fringe is smooth, putting may well be the choice. If not, the simple chip-putt will give you the best of both worlds – a chip that reacts like a putt.

All you have to do is adopt your regular putting stance and grip, but play the ball back of centre (opposite your right toe), ease your weight forward and stand close to the ball. It's then a matter of making your regular putting action: focus on the gentle rocking of the shoulders and let the arms work naturally to work the club back and forth with a simple pendulum-like stroke. Keep your head still, and nip the ball forwards. The follow through should be nice and short to ensure solid contact.

Most experts agree that the best strategy is to carry the fringe just onto the green and let the ball run to the hole from that point just like a putt. Club selection is the only other variable you have to consider: A short shot from above the hole is best played with a lofted club (say a 9-iron or a wedge) that will get the ball to hop and run slowly just a few feet. But if you face a fairly long and slightly uphill shot, you need a less lofted club, like a 7-iron, that will encourage the ball to 'run out' on the green. Go down the shaft a couple of inches as you make your grip (that enhances your feel), and keep your body still as your shoulders and arms control the movement of the club. You want softness in your hands, but no wrist action to speak of.

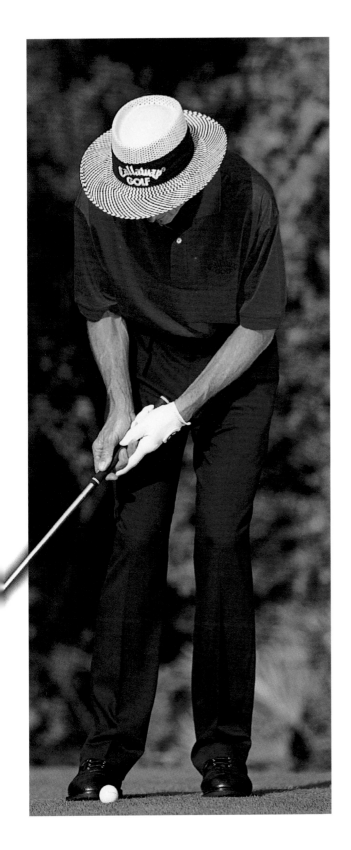

The regular chipping stroke (and a hint of wrist action)

Few shots in golf offer the versatility of the chip-putt, but its use is limited to the very fringes of the green. A yard or two off the putting surface, at most. But as you get a little further from the green, so the chip-putt must give way to the regular chipping action. Again, this technique has its origins in the putting stroke, but extended now to feature a subtle wrist action that imbues a silky-smooth quality to the motion, and one that allows you to create a little more speed through impact to achieve more distance and manipulate the flight of the ball.

When you look at the regular chipping stroke in the context of the short game family, it follows the natural progression. The basic motion is again engineered from the upper body, the secret being to blend in the rhythmic swinging of the hands and arms. Within that framework you can then introduce the wrist action I talked about a moment ago to both heighten your sense of feel and enable you to accelerate the club into the back of the ball. Again, it all revolves around the set-up, and with a fairly narrow but open stance, this simple reminder will keep you

on the right track: *Ball back, hands forward, weight forward.* That simple advice will help you to achieve a set-up that effectively primes the action. There is no real turning motion of the body to speak of, so get your feet close together and lean towards the target. (You will be standing further from the ball than with the chip-putt method.) One final tip is to sense that your upper arms rest lightly on your chest – that promotes the good 'linkage' of arms and body we have spoken about.

Once you are comfortable, all you have to do is rock the shoulders to bring your stroke to life. Let the pendulum theory take over. Gently rock your shoulders and let your arms and hands respond to their momentum. Sense that your control comes from the centre of your upper body as you move the club back and forth; though 'alive' and sensitive to the stroke, the hands and wrists should not be overly active. A light grip pressure keeps the hands and arms in touch with the flow of the stroke, and you should be aware of a little flexing in the wrists as you change direction from backswing to downswing (more in response to the weight of the clubhead than anything else). That subtle action is all it takes to add a silky touch to your stroke. Having pinched the ball off the turf, the follow through should ideally be a little shorter than the backswing – a little turn of the body through the ball encourages rhythm – and as ever it's advisable to hold your finish.

Hint of wrist action adds that silky-smooth rhythm that all good chippers of the ball have in common.

Higher...lower...longer...shorter

The sheer variety of shots that you face around the green demands that you experiment with your chipping action to hit the ball high, bump it low, make it run and make it stop. Controlling the speed of the delivery is a key variable that you have to understand, and that involves varying the length and the tempo of your stroke. Swinging the hands to about waist high would be the maximum for a chip shot (anything beyond that and you're in pitching territory), and fine-tuning your wrist action controls the acceleration into the back of the ball.

This is something you simply have to practice. Club selection is another obvious variable to tinker with (along with the ball position within your stance) to produce shots of a varying trajectory. The lower the number on the iron, the lower the loft and the more the ball will want to run when it lands on the green. The more lofted the club, the higher the ball flies and the less it will be inclined to run on the green. Go out and see what you can do. Just remember that on every shot your hands must lead the clubhead to a controlled finish. That's the sign of a well-executed stroke. Keep it in mind also that good players always aim to land the ball on the putting surface – that way the first bounce and subsequent run is more predictable.

Drill: How to achieve the perfect strike

You can tell a good chipper of the ball by the way he 'nips' the turf with a fairly aggressive action, controlling the initial reaction of the ball on the green with a touch of backspin before it 'releases' and runs out to the hole. To highlight these qualities in your own stroke, try these simple drills. The first requires that you place a club on the ground six inches behind the ball you intend to hit, and then work on your stroke until you can miss the shaft both on the way back and

on the way down into impact. As you set-up to the ball (which has to be back in the stance), ease your weight towards the target, and keep it there throughout. Rocking the shoulders and swinging the arms in harmony will then reward you with a stroke that lifts the clubhead over the shaft going back before pinching into the turf as you collect the ball on the way through. The more you practise this, the more you will fine-tune the descending angle of approach that you need to achieve this desired ball-turf strike, which is so important in terms of your ability to control the distances effectively.

To further reinforce this action, I also recommend that you practise hitting shots with your right heel raised a couple of inches off the ground. That encourages you to keep your weight on the left side throughout, which immediately gives you a feeling of being slightly ahead of the ball through impact. This drill is basically designed to ensure that your hands lead the clubface into the ball to deliver a firm and slightly descending strike as opposed to the scoopy action that plagues so many golfers.

Remember, all short-game skills rely heavily on the set-up. Keep this legend fixed in your mind: *Ball back, hands forward, weight forward.* For you cricket lovers out there, the set-up is a bit like the position you would take to the crease with a bat in your hands. Standing comfortably open to the target line, you settle the majority of your weight on your left side, and ease your upper body, your hands and knees towards the target. What you are doing, in effect, is pre-setting impact. All you have to focus on is gently rocking the upper body to create the simple pendulum-type action that accelerates the clubhead into the back of the ball, and hold your finish with the hands below waist high. Encouraging a little 'play' in the wrists adds that element of flow that keeps the stroke oiled.

Remember, for solid contact the hands must always lead the clubhead through impact.

• PITCHING •

When it came to designing my Academy headquarters at Champions' Gate in Florida, one of the things I was most excited about was the pitching area. The short-game is all about distance control, and this facility, with small sand-target greens scattered over a range of between 30 and 80 yards, offers students the perfect opportunity to fine-tune all aspects of their wedge game. And believe me, it sees a lot of business.

Pitching the ball tests your ability to make and repeat what is basically a mini-swing, but without the power associated with a full turn and release of body

speed. It's a 'part shot', and, like the chipping action, it's governed by the turning motion of the upper body over the support of the knees and thighs. It's very much an 'up-and-down' action, the lie-angle of the wedge and sand iron promoting what is naturally the steepest swing of them all. Back in the opening chapters of the book, I identified the correct 'setting' of the wrists as the key to making a good swing, and that same action plays a key part here, also. The length of the swing (and the distance you fly the ball) is governed by the amount of turn in the upper body, while the wrists keep the clubhead swinging up and down on a good plane, returning the natural loft to the ball at impact.

The basic pitch – a swing in miniature

Let me take you through the basic pitching swing in more detail. Here I have a regular shot of 50 yards or so, and I have selected a sand iron. The set-up sees my feet open to the ball-to-target line, while my hips and shoulders remain square (i.e. parallel with the target line). The ball is played in the middle of my feet, and as I flex my knees for that vital sense of stability in the lower body, I am also conscious of easing my weight forwards onto my left side.

These are the basic rules of engagement when you set up to play a shot inside full swing distance. What you must remember is that a pitch is not a full swing, and thus does not allow you to create the dynamics necessary for your body to rotate and clear through impact. So you have to pre-set that position. That explains the slightly open stance as you ease your way into the shot. When you are ready to make your swing, the key is then to turn your upper body over the support of the knees and thighs, and work on swinging the club up on plane with a good wrist action, setting the club up on end as you swing to a comfortable three-quarter position.

When you work on these shots, always look for this halfway-back 'set' position. Waggle the clubhead to this point to free-up your hands, wrists and forearms. This checkpoint holds the key to a regular swing, and here it again confirms that you have the club swinging up on a good plane. Maintain a light grip pressure and the weight of the clubhead will automatically set the wrists for you. As the club swings up on end, it will actually feel quite light in your hands in this near-vertical position. That's a good sign you are on track. Looking from this angle, the hands should appear to be just about in the middle of your chest. This confirms that the arms and the body are working *together*, and, such is the symmetry in a good swing that the follow-through mirrors this position as you release the club and face the target.

Another good swing thought – and one that encourages a 'syrupy' rhythm – is to get your stomach in motion. Turn your centre away from and then towards the target. That will create the momentum that you need to get your arms and the clubhead swinging freely and smoothly. Then it's a matter of adjusting the length of your swing to control the length of the shot.

Turn back, turn through. Allied with a good wrist action, this motion is the key to crisp pitch shots.

Drill: Umbrella gets you swinging on track!

The best lesson I can give you to improve wedge technique concerns this issue of swing plane, specifically hingeing (or 'setting') the wrists in the early stages of the backswing to swing the club up on end. Just as I explained in the earlier chapters on full swing technique, this really holds the key to your ability to create a repeating swing that returns the clubface squarely to the ball. And this simple drill can really help you to appreciate the sensation of swinging the club up and down on plane.

Take an umbrella and stand it vertically in the ground about a foot outside your right heel. The trick now is to focus on using the wrists properly so that you hinge the club up and miss the umbrella on the

way back (for the first few shots most golfers will whack the umbrella). In a few minutes this simple drill will encourage you to swing the club up on a fairly vertical plane – as it should given its natural lie angle at address. After working on the backswing, move the umbrella to a position just outside your front foot (see over the page) to check that the through-swing mirrors that same vertical plane. As you release the club the wrists hinge the club up once again on its way to the finish. The beauty of this drill is that it simplifies the mechanics involved, leaving you to enjoy the sensation of the swing as you hit shots. Relax, and feel the hands leading the clubhead as you accelerate through impact, taking ball then turf for a crisp strike.

Swinging on the plane!

Stick an umbrella in the ground to remind you of the importance of swinging the club up and down on a good natural plane – and in a short time you will enjoy striking crisp pitch shots.

DAVID LEADBETTER

DAVID LEADBETTER

The wedge game – How to fine-tune your distance control

Once you have a feel for this controlled and easy swing, go out and work on finding your best distances with each of your wedges. That's the first step in building a solid wedge game. With a standard wedge, a comfortable full swing should give you a pitching distance of around the 100 yard mark, depending on your natural swing speed. We all have different physical capabilities. Your middle wedge (sometimes referred to as a Gap wedge) might give you a shot of 75 yards, while your most lofted sand iron might fly, say, 50 yards. The exact distance is not the issue. What matters most of all is that you are able to repeat a comfortable swing and have the ball travel a certain distance with each of these clubs. Find a personal scale that you can relate to, and then use that information out on the course.

As for fine-tuning the 'in-between' distances, there are a number of options to experiment with. For starters, try going down the shaft progressively by one, two or even three inches. With every step you take you effectively shorten the length of the shaft, which means that without having to adjust your swing you automatically slow down your speed through the ball and hit shots that fly less through the air. Each time you shorten your grip you might also narrow your stance a fraction, and move the ball back, towards your right foot. These adjustments add to your versatility in playing different length shots.

Experimenting with the ball position within your stance is one of the easiest and most effective ways to adjust the height and the trajectory of your pitch shots: run the scale – play it back to punch the ball low, forward to cut it up high with maximum loft.

Perfect distance – every time! Swinging your hands and arms to imaginary points on a clockface is the easiest way to vary the length of your swing and subsequent speed through the ball.

Another good way to control your pitching swing is to think in terms of matching numbers on a clock-face. Swing back to 9 o'clock and through to 3 o'clock. Then a little further, from 10 o'clock to 2 o'clock. A full pitching swing would be from 11 o'clock to 1 o'clock. Within this framework you can also vary the trajectory of your shots simply by adjusting the ball position. Don't be afraid to work the scale. If you want to hit a lower shot, move the ball back in your stance and keep your weight on your left side. To play a higher shot, open your stance a little more, move the ball forward, and settle your weight more evenly between your feet. This is all part of the fun of practice – remember, never attempt a shot on the course unless you have practised it. Because it shares the key elements of technique, working on your pitching will benefit your regular full swing too.

To practise distance control by varying the length of your swing, the backswing and through-swing should be approximately equal in length.

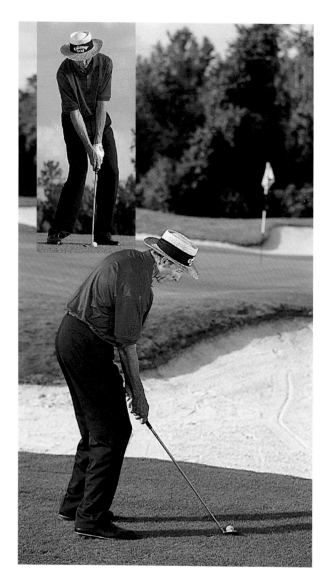

Keep hands and arms 'soft' to lob the ball

In the course of your experiments around the green, one shot will appeal more than perhaps any other: the lob. You've seen this on TV – often described as the 'Phil Mickelson' shot, given that the left-hander is so adept at lofting the ball almost vertically with a sand iron and stopping it within a few feet on the green. It takes a great deal of confidence to pull this off on the course, and certainly it's a shot that you have to practise seriously before you attempt it. You

also need a pretty decent lie to slide the clubface under the ball, so don't be tempted by it if you find yourself on a bare or firm piece of turf.

With a decent lie, however, you can conjur up a shot that enables you to lob the ball over whatever may stand between you and the hole and have it stop very quickly on the green. The set-up adjustments are relatively simple, though you do need to practise them to build confidence. To start, stand with your

body open in relation to the target (i.e. feet, knees, hips and shoulders aligned to the left of your target), but aim the clubface a little to the right (i.e. lay it open, just as you would do to play a regular sand shot). Position the ball in the forward part of your stance and settle your weight evenly between your feet. The technique itself demands that you keep the clubface open throughout the swing, crucially through the impact area. A soft pair of hands assist

you in swinging the club at a fairly leisurely pace, and you should feel that your backswing is fairly long and languid (not short and choppy). Let your arms control the motion and sense that your hands are 'dead' as you slide the clubface under the ball. The open stance will encourage a slightly out-to-in path that cuts across the ball, and though the clubface was aimed a little to the right, the line of your swing sees to it that the ball pops up on target.

• SAND PLAY •

able to skim the clubhead through the sand in such a way that the flange acts as a rudder, literally 'bouncing' the clubhead (and the ball) out of the sand.

How do you get that bounce working in your favour? The answer lies in the set-up. And the first rule of greenside sand play is that you *pre-set the clubface before you grip the club and settle down to play the shot*. Holding the club up in front of your body, swizzle the grip through your fingers (turning the leading edge to the right), and then complete your grip. Once that adjustment is in place, complete your set-up with a fairly open stance (something in the region of 30 degrees is perfect), play the ball just forward of centre, and shuffle your feet into the sand for a firm base.

Once you understand this concept of 'bounce' and the thinking behind the set-up position, the mystery of sand play is over. All you have to do now is trust the club to do the job for which it is designed, swing along the line of your body and splash the clubhead through the sand. You certainly don't need to think about cutting across the ball or digging beneath it; you are aiming left of your target and swinging along the line of your toes will give you the slicing action that enables you to splash the ball out. Don't be afraid of being aggressive on these shots, either. The sand is a buffer, and absorbs the speed of the clubhead, so you have to make a fairly decent swing to have the ball come out only a short distance. For consistency, the key is to aim two or three inches behind the ball and take the same amount of sand on every shot. Then it's a fairly simple matter of adjusting the length and the speed of your swing to regulate the distance you fly the ball.

*T*aking a shallow cut of sand is the answer to good bunker play, and the modern sand iron is designed to help you do precisely that. If you take a close look at the heavy flange that characterizes its design, you will notice that the back edge of the flange sits appreciably lower than the leading edge. This gives the club a playing quality we call 'bounce', and utilizing that bounce is the key to playing good bunker shots. The trick is to understand how to go about reorganising your set-up so that you are

Sand drill: Thump...and listen

The rhythm of your swing plays a tremendous part in the quality of the strike through the sand. So much so that you can actually hear a good bunker shot. Next time you get a chance to practice, spend a few minutes swinging the club with your right hand only, and as you thump the sand, listen to the sound that you make. There's a certain sound attached to a good strike as the clubhead bounces through the sand – as opposed to the dull thud you get when it digs down too deeply.

The key to this right-hand drill is that you follow the usual set-up procedure. Take a slightly open stance, and rotate the clubface into an open position before gripping with the right hand. Then play away, utilizing that element of 'bounce' provided by the heavy flange on the sand iron, so that you remove a shallow divot as you release the the clubhead freely through impact. As long as you trust your swing, the back of the flange works as a rudder, literally bouncing the clubhead out. Experiment in different parts of the bunker, each time aiming to remove a shallow cut of sand as you swing the club on a nice wide radius and accelerate freely through impact.

Once you are able to skim the clubhead through the sand with your right hand, as a drill draw a line in the sand 2 to 3 inches behind the ball, and then aim to remove a divot of sand starting right on that line. Repeat this several times, aiming to take the same shallow cut of sand with each swing. See how accurate you can be with your striking, and then prepare to attempt some real shots (and bear it in mind that the rules of golf do not allow you to ground your club when setting up to the ball). Remember, you are not trying to hit the ball itself; your goal is to make contact with that imaginary line, whereupon the ball floats out on a cushion of sand. And when you execute these shots correctly you will hear a satisfying sound as the clubhead skims through the sand.

Spend the first few minutes of your practice session skimming the clubhead through the sand with your right hand only – then go after the same feeling when hitting shots, with both hands on the club.

Think RHYTHM, but be aggressive

One of the characteristics of good bunker players is that they make a fairly full swing, even when they only want to flop the ball out a short distance. They are confident and exhibit great rhythm and tempo, setting the club fairly early in the backswing with a full wrist action, and then turning their body all the way through the shot. That way they create the momentum necessary to splash the clubhead through the sand with some gusto. The longer the shot, the more upbeat the swing and the less sand they take (experiment aiming a little closer to the ball, say an inch); a shorter shot would be played with a lazier swing and a little more sand to cushion the blow at impact. These are the variables you have to experiment with.

Whenever you find yourself experiencing bouts of inconsistency out of greenside bunkers, go back to the basics and evaluate your rhythm. In my experience, players who struggle to play these shots with any confidence are often guilty of making too short a backswing, which is then followed by a jerky downswing and a 'stab' at the sand. The result is that the club is simply not accelerating through the sand, and the 'bounce' fails to kick in. If this sounds familiar, remind yourself to make a full backswing and mirror-image that with a full follow-through.

Make a long, *flowing* swing

Though you only want the ball to travel a short distance, it is vital that you make a relatively long swing, one that generates sufficient speed through impact to splash the clubhead through the sand

HELP! Take the wrists out of the equation

Top players make bunker shots look easy, but there's no question that if you struggle to escape the sand you can soon become embroiled in a mental tussle with yourself as confidence ebbs away. To get around that, here's an alternative theory; basically, it involves taking the wrists out of the equation altogether.

You set-up to the ball in pretty much the same manner as I demonstrated for the regular technique (including opening the face before completing your grip) but then make a swing without breaking or hingeing the wrists at all. Play the ball this time a little more in the middle of the stance, (and make that a wider stance than normal), and swing with 'dead' wrists. Keep the triangle of arms and shoulders intact as you swing back and through on a wide arc – legs still – chest moving aggressively. That will produce the shallow swing that slices the open clubface through the sand beneath the ball. There will inevitably be a little 'lag' in the hands and wrists as you change direction, but your swing thought is to keep them out of the equation. That will reward you with a fool-proof technique to escape greenside bunkers in one shot, which is the main goal, after all.

Tough bunker shot? Experiment with a 9-iron

Just because it is stamped 'sand wedge' on the sole of the club doesn't mean you have to use it every time you find yourself in a greenside bunker. On those awkward distances of 20 to 40 yards, a 9-iron can often prove to be a much more effective option. The thinking behind this is that with less loft, the 9-iron provides more forward momentum than a sand wedge. At the set-up, opening the clubface in the usual manner (i.e. laying the face in the desired open position before you complete your grip) provides you with a sufficient degree of 'bounce' to prevent the club digging into the sand too deeply. After that, it's a

relatively simple matter of applying the regular greenside bunker technique to produce a shot that flies considerably further than would a sand wedge. Just bare it in mind that the ball will tend to run a little more on landing – although that, of course, can prove to be a bonus in getting the ball up to the hole.

CHAPTER

Simple reminders
for great golf

KEY THOUGHTS AND PHRASES
THAT WILL HELP YOU TO IMPROVE
IN ALL AREAS OF THE GAME

One question I get asked more than any other is: 'How can I become a more consistent golfer?' That's the ultimate challenge for all who play this game. It doesn't matter if I am working with a tour player or an avid 'weekender' struggling to break 100 – every golfer has at some time or other asked himself why he cannot produce his best golf all the time. Or at least more often. How do you turn occasional bursts of skill into your regular performance? What do you have to do to eliminate the disaster shots that ruin a good round? Is there a secret to striking the ball on the course as well as you strike it on the range? In short, how do you repeat a solid

swing and play to your potential for all 18 holes? Developing a swing you can trust to get you safely from A to B is the first step in learning to play this game. After that it's all down to practice, and your experience of different playing conditions.

It all depends what you want to get out of this game. Some work harder than others, but clocking up the hours on the practice tee is no guarantee of success. This is why so many players struggle when they move from a practice tee environment and on to the golf course. All of a sudden, instead of a wide open range to aim at there are now trees and hazards, out of bounds and water, and they fall into the trap of

trying to 'over-control' the situation. The world is full of good ball strikers who haven't a clue how to apply their skills to cope with the challenges thrown up on the course; equally, there are players who may only be average ball-strikers, but who more than make up for that with exceptional course management and short-game skills. These are the golfers who win competitions and score consistently.

Positive thoughts and clear, realistic thinking. That's really what playing good golf is all about. With common sense, you can actually think your way to a better game. If you head out on to the course with a million different ideas buzzing around inside your head, don't be surprised if you're having trouble unravelling your swing. You are simply not giving yourself the opportunity to play to your potential. And you are certainly not helping yourself to improve and move your game forwards. For better and more consistent ball-striking, the solution is to be aware of just one or two positive swing thoughts (or 'keys') that help you to repeat a good motion automatically, without you actually having to think so hard about it that you get tied in knots.

The best tips in golf are always the simplest ones – the throwaway one-liners. It's very rare that I will have a player call me up and say, 'You know, David, that complicated mechanical stuff we talked about for a couple of hours last week has really helped my game.' But what I do hear a lot of is how a simple piece of imagery, or a particular swing thought, made a world of difference. Usually basic stuff concerning the set-up, the first move away from the ball, and so on. The reason these bite-size reminders work so well is that they give you something that is easy to grasp and positive to focus on. They help to create the muscle memory you need to create a certain movement under pressure. And that's the reason you practise in the first place – so that you can forget about technique on the course.

My advice to you is go out and experiment with all of the following reminders, improvement drills and random thoughts to find which ones are best suited to you and your game. There's a whole mix of stuff here, and concentrating on one or two of these ideas when you play or practise (or just swing a club out in the garden) will make you a better golfer for the simple reason it will stop you worrying about a hundred other things – and that in itself is usually enough to inspire a better all-round motion. Entertaining positive thoughts about the swing in every situation from tee to green will give you the means to repeat the good habits that allow you to hit solid shots, and, over time, making them as automatic as possible.

I mentioned at the start of this book that I tend to be regarded as a technical coach. Hopefully by now you appreciate what I like to describe as the 'common sense simplicity' behind my methods. If not, perhaps this closing compendium of thoughts will convince you once and for all that golf is really not complicated at all. I hope you have fun putting them to the test.

• WARMING UP •

Get your engine started

At just about every level, golf is becoming a much more athletic sport, which explains why young players these days are hitting the ball such astonishing distances. Such is my interest in this aspect of learning that the David Leadbetter Academy sites around the world are all affiliated with fitness instructors who devise training programmes for strength and flexibility, but you don't have to be a potential world-beater to take on board some of the basic ideas that we work on. I'm not about to prescribe a rigorous training schedule for you to pin up on the wall of your office, but for the sake of your game I do hope that you at least set aside a little time to run through these stretching exercises in readiness to make some good swings. Do each exercise a few times – the 5 minutes you spend will be more than worthwhile.

● **Arch** your trunk: Taking the ends of a club in each hand, raise your arms high above your head and stretch your body to its fullest extent. Be as tall as you can be. Then, slowly arch your torso from side to side, holding the extended positions for at least a count of three – feel the muscles in your torso stretch.

● **Stretch** your legs: Hands on hips, take a big step forward and gradually lower your weight on to the support of the thigh muscles. Hold the position for a few seconds, then repeat on the other side. This will get the blood flowing through the legs and generally prepare the thigh and calf muscles to play the stabilizing role.

● **Turn** your shoulders: Hook your right arm under your left elbow and pull on it as you turn to create your backswing coil. Feel the stretch in your torso.

⬤ **Adopt** the basic 'pivot drill': Good players move their body well, and this drill will encourage just that. Take your posture, hook a club across your shoulders, and work on turning your upper body back and then through, as you would to make a swing. The key is to maintain your body angles (particularly your spine angle) as you turn your shoulders through a full 90 degrees, both on the way back and the way through, and shift your weight in tandem with the backswing and throughswing motion.

● **Practise** the two-club swing: Hold two clubs together (three if you're feeling energetic) and swing them together in slow motion. The combined weight of the clubheads will create an irresistible momentum that will soon have you winding and unwinding your swing freely. As you make a full turn in both directions, you want to feel the arms and hands work in harmony with the body.

• ON THE PRACTICE TEE •

Get a sense of impact, and repeat it

Good ball strikers return the back of the left hand squarely at impact. That's how they create backspin and flight their shots consistently. They strike the ball with real authority. The back of the left hand leads (and mirrors) the clubface at impact, the right wrist firm, totally committed to the shot, the weight on the left foot and the left leg braced to absorb impact (hence the expression to 'hit into a firm left side').

As I suggested in chapter 2, it's a good idea from time to time to actively re-create the sensation of a good impact position when you practise. On the range at my academies we use these impact bags, which allow a student to hit hard against the resistance it provides to fully experience the sensations involved. As an alternative, the same effect can be achieved quite easily if you find something firm to press against (the base of your golf bag as it is lying on the ground), and slowly exert and increase the pressure with a mid iron. Hold this 'braced' position for a few seconds between shots, and take a moment to reflect on exactly what you are trying to achieve as the clubhead meets the ball.

When you get back into hitting shots for real, the trick then is to make this posed position your starting point, and try to duplicate that sensation of impact as you hit the shot. Once you get a sense of what a good impact position feels like, I think you'll find that you are able to return to it more easily...and more often. And hit better shots as a result.

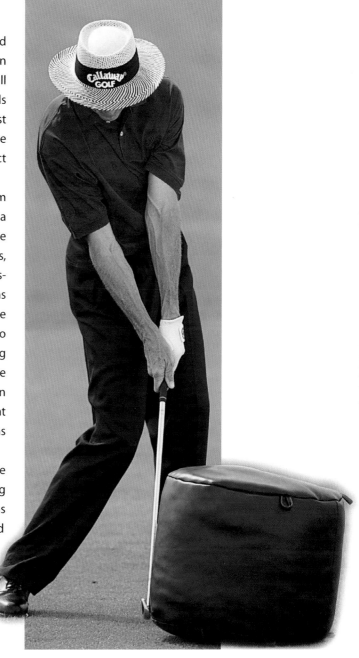

• THE FINAL COUNTDOWN •

Take a 'virtual' tour of the course

Many of the players that I work with like to round off their warm-up session on the practice tee with what I describe as a 'virtual reality' tour of the golf course they are about to play. It works like this: they look at the yardage chart and find, for example, that the first hole is a relatively short par four. After studying the layout of the hole, noting the trouble, they might decide that the smart shot is a 3-wood into the safe side of the fairway. So they tee-up a ball and play that shot, going through their routine just as they would do for real in a tournament. Then, based on the flight and anticipated outcome of the shot, they figure out where the ball might have finished, calculate the yardage to the green and select the club to play the next shot. And so it goes on. In ten minutes they may well have played the first nine holes – both physically *and* mentally. And there's the rub. This type of visualization prepares you for the reality of the course, improving your mind-set and familiarizing you with the shots that you will soon need to produce for real.

• JUST A THOUGHT... •

Open your mouth, relax your jaw, and breathe

This may amuse you, but look around and you'll see a lot of people who keep their lips so tightly pursed at the set-up that they actually forget to breathe. This creates an inner tension that builds and builds to the inevitable detriment of the swing. So, next time you play, remind yourself to open your mouth and relax the muscles in your neck and shoulders as you stand over the ball. Take a deep breath, and then, as you let it go, sense that wave of relaxation spread over your body, leaving you ready to *swing* the clubhead.

This technique works with every club in the bag, all the way from the driver to the putter. Any time you feel tight or anxious, it really is a great way to banish nervous tension. As you address the ball, breathe in deeply through your nose and feel your chest expand. Then exhale out through your mouth just prior to starting your backswing (or putting stroke). I have lost count of the number of students over the years who have used this on the course to forget about mechanics and recapture lost tempo. Once you achieve that inner 'softness' at address, you will start to swing in a relaxed fashion, and from that moment on everything will benefit.

• SWING KEY •

For stability, keep that gap between your knees

One of the cornerstones of my thinking on the swing is that the lower body provides a resistance to the turning motion of the torso. That's what gets the swing 'loaded up' like a spring, ready to unwind in the downswing. A problem I see all too often is that of the

lower body (knees and feet) being so active on the backswing that they don't offer any effective resistance to the top half.

Think about the dynamics you are trying to achieve. Ideally, you want to coil your upper body against the athletic resistance of the lower body. To do that the knees and thighs have to be braced, and maintaining this gap between the knees is a pretty good indication of a strong lower body action. In the process of winding and turning, your left knee may move in just a little, and the right knee may rotate slightly, but basically you want the same gap at the top of the swing that you had at address.

Placing a ball between the thighs is a great way to appreciate this sense of stability in the lower body, and from time to time you should use it as a reminder of the importance of keeping the legs 'quiet'. The key is to maintain that flex in the right knee as you turn against it (and in so doing you should be aware of some pressure in the right thigh). That creates the coil that puts the speed in your swing and the power in your shots. If the right leg straightens during the course of the swing, or the left knee shoots forwards, you are going to lose that vital stability in the lower body. And with it your ability to coil effectively.

A lot of people ask about whether the left heel should be allowed to lift to complete the backswing. I only recommend that to players who lack flexibility. Otherwise the best advice to most golfers is keep the left foot planted, so that as you turn you really feel the 'stretch' in the midriff and upper body. That will also serve to keep your swing shorter, more compact, and easier to repeat. With the driver, a full turn of the upper body may, in some cases, pull the left foot up off the ground. If that's what's necessary to reach the top, so be it. Just make sure you don't encourage any independent or superfluous movement in the legs.

• RHYTHM & TEMPO •

For rhythm, try the two-step drill

Along with a sense of turning and coiling your body in the process of making a good swing, it is vital that you appreciate how your weight moves (a better expression is that it *flows*) as you turn back and through. Essentially, it moves into your right side as you swing away from the ball and then across and into your left side as you unwind your swing to a finish. A logical progression. But you need to work on it.

Failing to shift your weight correctly upsets the overall rhythm of your swing, and costs you power. If that's hurting your game, try this simple two-step drill to improve this element of your swing. Sit the ball up on a tee, and start with your feet close together. Then, on the count of 'one', move your right foot away from the left and at the same time make your backswing. As you reach the top, lift your left foot off the ground, and on the count of 'two' step smoothly into your downswing, this time moving the left foot back towards the target to provide the trigger to starting down and swinging through. Work on this until the two halves of your swing blend into one continuous motion. You should be aware of a distinct feeling of lateral movement as you move back and forth, almost as if you were dancing with the club.

Rehearse this as often as you can (tag it to the end of your warm-up routine). In a very short space of time it will help you to increase your acceleration into the ball, which will increase your clubhead speed. Imagine the ball simply gets in the way – that focuses your attention on swinging *through* the shot. Swing to the finish, and make sure when you get there that your weight is supported on your left side, your right shoulder pointing at the target.

Like a dance move, the two-step drill will get the club, your arms and body working in harmony, and with a rhythm that virtually repeats itself.

· IRON PLAY ·

For consistency, swing shorter

I talked about this in chapter 3, but the message is worth repeating: there is no doubt in my mind that most golfers would improve their ball striking overnight if they were to just swing the club with a shorter and more compact action.

It's no secret that most amateurs tend to underclub and then swing too hard, which more often than not results in a poor contact with the ball. (Women don't tend to be so caught up in the 'what club did you hit' syndrome, but because they are more supple, and in many cases capable of turning the hips almost as far as the shoulders, they do have a problem in that their swing gets too long and too loose.) To counter these difficulties, I suggest keeping the feet flat on the ground as much as possible as a direct means of restricting your hip turn, which will basically tighten up the coil in the backswing and give you a much more consistent position at the top. If you are guilty of swinging the club too far, or simply experiencing bouts of inconsistency with your irons, try one or all of these remedies:

Restricting yourself to a three-quarter length swing with the mid- to short irons will produce solid shots more often.

● **Grip** the club a little more firmly with the last three fingers on the left hand. Losing the security of the left hand grip at the top is a common fault that leads to a 'hanging' overswing. Reinforcing the security of the left hand with the last three fingers will immediately firm things up.

● **Keep** your feet flat on the ground during the backswing. That will help to restrict the turning motion of the hips, which should increase the resistance they provide to the motion of the upper body, and thus tighten up your backswing coil.

● **Try** to imagine at address that you are standing in the middle of a clockface. Swing your arms to no further than 11 o'clock on the backswing. The more compact you make your swing, the more it is likely to 'repeat'.

• IMPROVE YOUR RHYTHM •

For better rhythm, swish the grip

Every golfer wants to improve the quality of his technique, but there's no such thing as one perfect swing. The human element just doesn't allow it, which is why it's so important to concentrate on repeating the swing you do have with a rhythm that allows you to get the most out of it – *in other words finding the perfect swing for you*. You have to swing at a tempo that gives all of the pieces of the puzzle time to fit together to produce the maximum clubhead speed at impact. Above all else, you have to swing the club at a speed you can control.

Great players have the ability to swing with a rhythm that disguises all manner of flaws they may have, and as a result they tend to repeat good impact habits (even when they are playing poorly, maintaining a good rhythm is what enables these players to

minimize the damage and get the ball around the course). Likewise, the easier you swing the club the better you will strike the ball.

One way to recapture lost rhythm, either on the range or out on the course, is to flip the club around, grip the head and swish the shaft. Because the club now feels extremely light in your hands you will find that you immediately begin to swing more slowly (the majority of amateur players apply too much effort), and this will remind you of the need to sequence your swing correctly and build up your acceleration *gradually* in order to create the loudest noise through the impact area. As you rehearse this drill, concentrate your focus from 'pocket-to-pocket': i.e. give it a rip from the time your hands reach the right pocket on the way down all the way to the left pocket on the way through. That's the only place in the swing where clubhead speed actually matters.

• FULL SWING •

Use your head, and 'turn'

'Keep your head still' – possibly the worst phrase in golf. Full of good intention, in that no one should be encouraged to move their head about excessively during the swing, but damaging because a good swing must inevitably involve a little head movement to accommodate a full turn of the shoulders and upper body. In most good swings the head will tend to move 'off' the ball – particularly with the longer shafted clubs. To stand over the ball and think about *not* moving the head actually inhibits the good upper body motion that is involved in making a full turn.

What you have to remember is that a good swing involves the *whole* body; if your hips or shoulders fail to turn and play their part, the hands and arms will be forced to take over, and when that happens you're on a one-way street to a weak and inconsistent swing. To check that your head is moving correctly, simply stick a pen in your mouth and watch it turn to the right as you start your backswing. (In fact, make sure first of all that your head is angled slightly to the right, away from the target. Focusing on the back of the ball with your left eye will help you to establish the right position.) Now ease your head gently to the right as you turn your shoulders, and sense your weight shifting across and on to your right side.

In freeing-up your head and body, you improve the turning motion of the torso generally. And that will help you to create a better backswing coil, one that promises the recoil action that creates speed on the way back down. So, don't be concerned if your head moves a little to accommodate that action. It's perfectly acceptable. The best players in the world do it.

• THE MIND GAME •

Nothing but routine business

Years ago, in his book *How to Play Your Best Golf All the Time*, which is still one of my favourite general texts on golf, Tommy Armour wrote that the game is divided into three tasks: you play strokes, the course and the opponent. To those observations I am inclined to add a fourth category, in that you also have to play yourself. And conquering the 'mental chess' that goes on in the mind of a golfer over 18 holes is quite possibly the toughest hurdle of all.

The following rules will help to keep your head clear:

● **Develop** and trust a pre-shot routine: Every great player follows a routine that standardizes his actions on the course. Nothing is left to chance, and this is something you have to incorporate into your own game. Work on this on the practice tee, so that on the golf course it is as instinctive as your swing. Your all-consuming focus is the target. Stand behind the ball and take a good look at the shot before you move in to play. Visualise the ball flying through the air, homing in on the target. Success. And always narrow your focus, picking out the smallest target possible – whether it be a leaf on a tree or a patch of grass ahead of the ball. The more you clarify your focus, the more in tune your body will be with it – it's called *reacting* to the target.

● **One** key thought: As far as swing thoughts go, one key thought is all you need to take with you on to the golf course. Find a positive swing key that inspires good motion, and stick with it. Too many technical thoughts will only create confusion and – ultimately – tension. One positive thought is all you need.

● **You** have shots…so use them! Unrealistic expectations can put you and your game under pressure. If you are an 18-handicapper, your personal par is not a standard 72, it's 90. So, assuming two putts per hole, that means you are allowed two shots to reach a par three, three to reach a par four and four to reach a par five. That's the wonderful thing about the handicapping system – it enables you to play your own game and enjoy your own personal successes, depending on your ability. Next time you play, spend a couple of minutes looking at the card, calculate your 'personal par', and formulate a strategy based on your handicap. Set yourself a realistic goal and not only do you take the pressure off, but you'll probably achieve it. And get more enjoyment out of your game.

● **Play** your own game!: The more time you can spend in the company of better players, the more their skill and 'course management' skills will rub off on your game. But don't make the mistake of trying to keep up with someone who may be a longer hitter than you. Stick to your own personal tempo. Play your own game, and repeat a smooth swing.

● **Play** a little 'notebook golf': To complement a yardage chart, a small notebook is the best prop you can take out on to the golf course. Write down personal distance markers, and make a note of the clubs you use from certain points on the fairway. Any other positive details you can record will help you next time you go out. Making notes is a good habit to get into, as doing so focuses your mind on your game – and that's what good golf is all about.

• TOUGH LIES I •

Dealing with slopes

One thing I stress to all my students is that you *play* a golf course, you don't fight it. You have to work with the lie of the land, use humps and hollows to gather the ball and feed it towards your target. Golf would be a dull game indeed if every course was flat, and learning to cope with slopes and uneven lies is all part of the fun. What you have to understand is that you cannot argue with the laws of physics. Instead, you have to factor them into your thinking.

Over the next few pages are four typical situations you have to deal with. In every single case it's up to you to create a set-up that enables you to go with the flow. Because balance is an issue, it's worth stating up front that on all these shots you are better off making what you feel is a three-quarter swing with the minimum amount of leg action. And remember, the ball will always tend to move in the direction of the slope.

Ball above the feet

A ball above the level of your feet has the effect of asking you to stand a little more upright at address, and raises the arms into a slightly more horizontal plane. The inevitable result is that you swing the club more *around* your body, which causes the ball to fly from right-to-left through the air. To allow for this you simply adjust your aim to the right of your target at the set-up. It's also a good idea to play the ball a little back in your stance. That way the clubface makes solid square contact with the ball.

For you slicers out there, practising with the ball above the level of your feet is great therapy that will replace your steep outside-to-in swing with a more shallow approach from the inside. It might even produce a draw...

Try this quick fix

As a drill, hitting shots with the ball a few inches above the level of your feet encourages a good turn and a powerful inside-to-out shaped release – the perfect antidote for players with a tendency to slice.

Ball below the feet

Any time you find the ball situated below the level of your feet, balance is the primary issue to deal with. The key is to use your legs like shock-absorbers, bending from the hips and flexing the knees to lower your centre of gravity and maintain balance as you place the club behind the ball. Spreading the feet a little wider apart than normal helps you get down to the shot, and adds to the stability in the lower body. But as a consequence of these adjustments, the body is in no position to turn effectively, and so you have to be prepared to make a more upright swing with the hands and arms. This leads to a tendency to cut across the ball through impact, so aim to the left of your target, and be prepared for the ball to drift from left to right through the air.

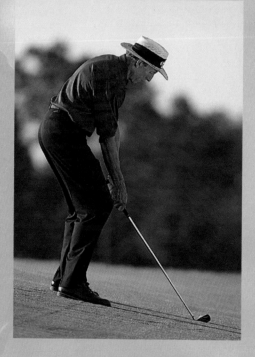

Use your knees as shock-absorbers to create a stable base that enables you to counter the slope and control your swing. Keep your feet as flat as possible for good balance.

Try this quick fix

If you have a problem hooking, hitting shots with the ball positioned a few inches below the level of your feet will promote a slightly steeper swing and a less pronounced in-to-out path through impact.

Uphill and downhill

The obvious factor to consider on an uphill lie (above) is that it naturally *enhances* the loft on the clubface. The upslope effectively acts as a launch pad, so the first thing to remember here is take at least one more club than the distance would ordinarily dictate. Then it's a matter of 'neutralizing' the effect of the slope as you set up to the ball. Get your body levels in tune with the gradient, so that you adopt what is basically a regular set-up inclined according to the conditions. Uphill your weight will naturally tend to fall on the lower foot, downhill it will go to the lower side. The

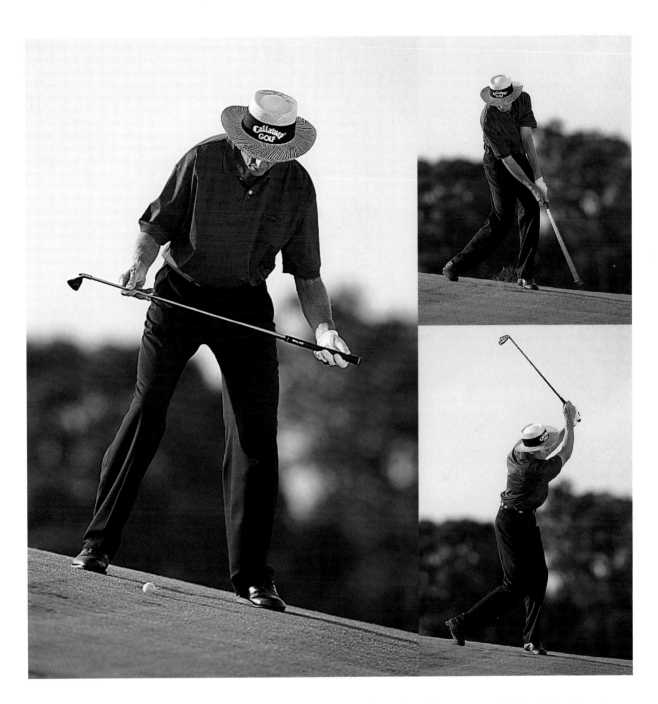

key is that it pretty well stays there throughout. Clearly, your balance is under threat, so keep the legs 'quiet' as you focus on making a controlled three-quarter swing. Another point here is that the uphill lie tends to restrict the follow-through, and the shot tends to become a fairly 'punchy' one. Downhill, the natural tendency is to want to lift the ball up, but the trick here (above) is to 'chase' after the ball and extend the clubhead down the slope as you release the whole of your right side. This time the ball is going to come out lower than normal, so take a more lofted club than the distance would usually require.

• TWO KEYS FOR A BETTER MOVEAWAY •

Get the butt-end of the club moving first

Some players focus so hard on getting the clubhead working away from the ball that they end up doing so with independent movement of the hands and arms. Others exacerbate the problem by picking the clubhead up with the hands, or whipping the clubhead inside from the word go. As a result, the natural radius of the swing is broken, and the coiling process is ruined before it has even begun.

One simple swing thought can help to solve all of these problems: focus on moving the butt-end of the club first. Do that and you will find that you actually get everything working away 'together'. Remember, the key to a solid swing lies in synchronizing the movement of the club, hands, arms and body; there has to be a harmony in this movement. So try this swing thought next time you go out to play: from the set-up position, try to get the butt-end of the club moving laterally (before the clubhead moves) and see if you don't maintain the shape of that triangle formed by your arms and shoulders as you engineer a smooth moveaway from the ball. The hands should pass close to the right thigh and your wrists will then hinge naturally to swing the club up on plane. And don't worry about the clubhead; wherever the butt-end goes, the head will eventually follow.

A sense of moving the butt-end of the club before the head has the effect of encouraging the hands, arms and club to move away together. Brushing away a second ball is another useful exercise, one that is designed to encourage width in the backswing.

DAVID LEADBETTER

• SWING KEY •

'Brush' the clubhead away

Moving the butt-end away is a good thought to have at the start of the backswing; another is to 'brush' the clubhead away from the ball. Particularly with the longer clubs that demand good width and radius for solid ball-striking, this helps you to achieve a lot of good things at the start of the swing: it keeps the clubhead travelling low to the ground and it creates a wide and smooth extension away from the ball. In that respect, it is also good for the overall rhythm of your swing.

As a drill, place a ball 12 inches or so behind the ball you are going to hit (and slightly inside the target line), and brush that ball away with the back of the clubhead as you make your backswing. Make sure that the butt-end of the club passes close to your right thigh, and that the clubhead stays low to the ground. Work on this for a few minutes and then hit a few shots with your driver, the ball teed up high. Think 'low, slow and wide', and you will get your swing properly 'loaded', the upper body coiling over the resistance of the lower body.

Another plus here is that starting your swing in this fashion also encourages you to move your weight across into your right side, which is so important, particularly with the longer clubs. Transferring your weight to the right and then to the left adds to the rhythm and momentum of your swing. And as your swing arc becomes wider, so you will produce a shallow sweeping action through the ball that results in square and solid contact.

• TOUGH LIES 2 •

Dealing with divots, hard pan and rough

Golf is anything but predictable, and the 'rub of the green' is not always going to be kind. When a ball is lying badly, the only way to guarantee moving it forwards with any degree of control is to 'squeeze' or punch it with a fairly steep downward blow, the hands always leading the clubhead through the strike. To achieve that it's usually a good idea to take a more lofted club than normal, choke down on the grip an inch or so (that enhances the wrist action for a steeper swing), play the ball back in your stance, and settle more of your weight on your front foot. All of these adjustments will help you to create a 'punchy'

three-quarter type swing characterized by this abbreviated follow through you see below.

Out of the rough, it all depends on your luck. If the ball is sitting well, you might be able to get anything at it – even a lofted fairway wood. But you have to be cautious. A relatively good lie such as this is prone to producing what's known as a 'flier'. This occurs when grass gets trapped between the clubface and the ball, causing it to skid off the face and fly much farther than normal. So you have to

Whether punching the ball from a divot, chasing it off the top of pine straw or moving it forward from thick grass, the hands must always lead the clubhead through impact.

be careful. Approaching a green, I always think it's better to come up a little short than risk flying the ball into whatever unknown hazards might be lurking through the back, so take a more lofted club. In very thick rough the only option is to take the shortest route back to the fairway – a ball-back-in-the-stance sand wedge job. Chop it out sideways. There's nothing else you can do.

Hardpan, pine straw or wood chipping? The solution is much the same. You have to do all you can to make clean contact, and a 'punchy' type of shot works best. Choke down on the grip, play the ball back in the stance, and sense that your left hand leads the club-face as you punch it forwards with a controlled three-quarter action. Remember, you are taking loft off the clubface, so be pre-pared for plenty of run, and make sure you avoid any trouble ahead of you – above all else get the ball back in play and make your next shot easier.

· STRATEGY ·

Any way the wind blows…

Let me give you some straight, practical advice to cope with playing in the wind:

● **First,** swing *easy*. The harder you try to hit the ball the more spin you generate and the more the ball will climb into a headwind, or deviate in a cross-wind. It takes considerable discipline to learn to control your swing in this fashion, but it's the only effective way to combat windy conditions. The easier you swing the club, the lower you flight the ball and the less it is affected. Along with this strategy, you must also learn to take at least one extra club (some player even prefer to take two more clubs and grip down the shaft for extra control). Even the slightest headwind knocks the ball down, so be prepared to 'club up', and get the ball to pin high. Also, never fight a cross-wind – always aim a little to the left or right, depending on the severity of the wind, and let the ball drift back on line.

● **Any** time the wind is behind you have to think carefully about your strategy. Standing on the tee you might well decide that a 3-wood is preferable to the driver. When the wind is with you, a 3-wood (or a long iron) may well provide all the distance you need with

much less a risk of missing the fairway. A tail-wind will inevitably cause the ball to run more than normal on landing, too, so factor that into the equation when you calculate the yardage to a certain part of the fairway, or the distance to a particular hazard. Stopping the ball is another problem approaching the green downwind. It is impossible to create much backspin, so you have to take less club and allow for the ball to run up to the flag.

What many players fail to understand is that a strong wind can have a dramatic affect on the behaviour of the ball around and on the green, also. In pitching and chipping you have to be aware that a headwind will cause the ball to stop much more quickly (even on those low bump-and-run shots), and that downwind, even with the most lofted wedges, it is virtually impossible to create 'stop' with backspin. The ball will creep forward, so adjust your thinking accordingly. Take these conditions into account when reading the greens, too. You might not think that the wind will do much to affect the line of a putt, but gusts can make a huge difference to the amount of borrow that you need to take, and indeed the pace at which you need to roll the ball. You may also have to take a wide stance to maintain your balance.

· TOUGH LIES 3 ·

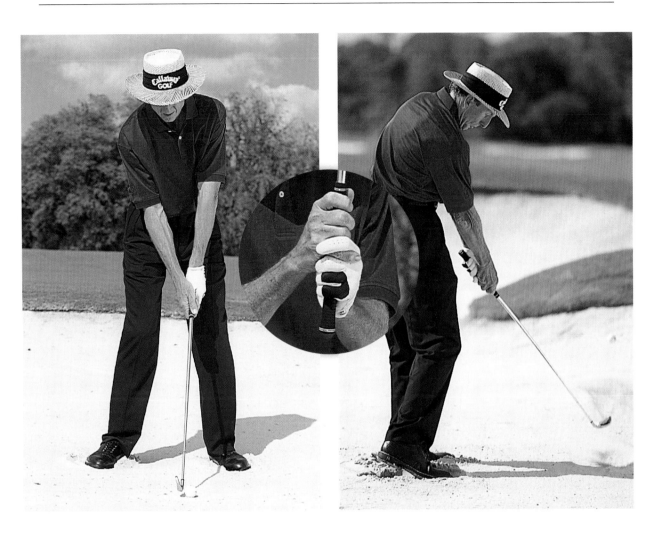

Clean getaway from a fairway trap

Any time you find your ball in a fairway bunker, the first thing you have to consider is the severity of the front lip. Your priority is getting the ball out of the bunker and back into play, so don't take unnecessary risks. Make a rule – *unless you are very skilled, never use a wood*. If the bunker is designed with a fearsome front lip, take a lofted club and take the safest route out to the fairway. Here, I've been lucky. This is a shallow bunker, and I can feel fairly confident playing a 5-iron. And the key to achieving good distance from this lie is to focus on striking the ball right on its equator. Grip the club a little shorter (you're basically encouraging a semi-thin shot), and roll your feet inwards to get the lower body well and truly 'anchored'. Excessive body movement is the biggest threat to pulling this shot off, so keep your lower body solid, and create the swing with a smooth hand, arm and shoulder motion. Playing the ball just forward of centre in your stance further encourages you to strike it cleanly on the equator.

• SHORT GAME •

Get out of jail with a fairway wood

You have probably seen the pro's use this little trick to get themselves out of an awkward spot around the green. A lot of players use a fairway wood to chip the ball from fluffy greenside rough, because the wide sole flattens the grass and makes good contact with the ball. Another opportunity presents itself here, where there is a steep slope to climb and you need a running shot. The fairway wood provides more forward momentum that a putter, and is less risky than an iron, which might dig into the turf. Gripping well down the shaft for extra feel, a putting type action produces a relatively short and easy-to-control stroke that gets the ball running willingly up the slope and onto the green. Give it a try.

DAVID LEADBETTER

A vivid imagination can produce all sorts of shots around the green – chipping the ball with a fairway wood being just one route of escape open to you.

· SAND PLAY ·

Plugged ball? Close the clubface

Given wet or firm sand conditions you would square up the clubface at the set-up to encourage more of a digging action at impact. You certainly don't want to encourage bounce – and neither do you when you find your ball buried in a real 'poached egg' lie, such as this. The only way to escape from here is to close the face dramatically as you set-up to the ball. Turn the toe in, and then focus on making a fairly steep back-swing and hitting down sharply into the sand just behind the ball. When you make contact, the clubface will be forced open and the ball will pop out in the ensuing explosion of sand. Don't worry about making a follow through, but remember that the ball will come out fairly hot, so you have to allow for a lot more run on the green than normal. Remember to take that into account when sizing up the shot.

• FAULT FIXING •

Slicers, keep the clubface looking at the ball

Especially for golfers who slice the ball, a good image to keep in mind on the backswing is that as you take the club back, you try to keep the clubface 'looking' at the ball for as long as you possibly can. A lot of people who slice are prone to 'rolling' (or 'fanning') the club during the first few feet of the backswing, which results in the clubface becoming open on its way to the top. (Then it's a matter of over-using the body in an attempt to square the clubface at impact, which usually results in swinging from out-to-in, and cutting across the ball.) But if you focus on keeping the clubface looking at the ball as you move it away (at least until the hands pass knee-high), you will find that as you reach the top, the clubface is square, or even slightly closed. With the clubface in this position you can then work on swinging back down to the ball from the inside, and make solid contact for straighter shots.

Square deal: if you have a tendency to slice, try to get the clubface 'looking' at the ball in the early stages of the swing.

• FULL SWING KEY •

Two thoughts for a better position at the top

Whenever he was asked what went through his head when he found himself under pressure, Jack Nicklaus would often say that his key swing thought was simply to 'complete' his backswing. Particularly with the driver, Jack's priority was to make sure that he made a full turn of his upper body to truly get behind the ball. In so doing, he enjoyed a better rhythm and the full benefit of a good body action.

Here are a couple of thoughts that can help you to achieve this desirable look at the top of the backswing. First, imagine that you simply turn your shoulders until the buttons on your shirt are directly over your right thigh. That will help you to guard against the common problem of failing to shift your weight (often related to keeping your head too still), and give you a good coil of the upper body. Another good swing thought is to work on getting your left thumb under the shaft at the top of your backswing (this is written for right-handed players; all you left-handers out there please read right for left!). If you can achieve this grip position at the top, you can be fairly confident that your wrists have hinged (or cocked) correctly, and that the club is now fully 'loaded' with energy.

Getting that thumb nicely under the shaft is also a good guarantee that the club is on line and 'in the slot' (i.e. parallel with the ball-to-target line). I mentioned earlier that maintaining the pressure in the last three fingers of your left hand also helps you to repeat a consistent position at the top, and it's worth repeating. Don't let the fingers work loose during the backswing. As Gary Player always liked to say, 'Make sure you *own* the club at the top of your swing.'

• SWING IMAGE •

Delayed wrist action provides the final thrust

If you were asked to pick up a ball and throw it as far as possible, my bet is you would create a hinge in your wrist as you loaded up your backswing, and then hold on to that angle until the very last moment, before unhinging to add that final thrust of acceleration to coincide with the release. The same principle applies to the golf swing: the wrists are seen to hinge in the process of 'loading' the backswing, and that angle is then retained deep into the downswing, until the centrifugal forces at work can be resisted no longer,

and the wrists deliver the final thrust of speed. All great players display this quality in their swing, and it's something you should think about next time you are out hitting balls – picture this wrist action, and apply the same dynamics to your swing. For solid ball-striking, it is vital that the hands do not release their energy too early ('casting' the club, or hitting from the top, are common power leaks). Remember, your objective is to release your maximum speed on the ball at impact, and to do that the wrists must retain their power until the very last possible moment – rather like cracking a whip, they then add the final burst of acceleration. Be patient.

• FAULT FIXING •

Slam the door on your slice!

Working from a slightly closed stance is good advice for anyone who tends to slice the ball from time to time. Pulling the right foot back just a few inches (but keeping the hips and shoulders square to your target line) actively encourages the right side of the body to turn out of the way on the backswing, which immediately improves the quality of the 'coiling' motion and gets the club swinging back on the desired inside path (senior golfers who lack flexibility would benefit from this). As a swing cue, simply turn your chest on top of your right leg. You are now in a position where you can swing down from the inside and freely release the club – and slam the door on your slice. In other words, shut the clubface on the ball by rotating your right forearm over the left through the impact area. Immediately after impact it should feel as if the back of the left hand is pointing at the ground. With a little practise this combination of thoughts and moves should enable you to replace your slice with a gentle draw.

If you are an habitual slicer of the ball, the problem may need more drastic surgery. Building on this image of 'slamming the door' on the ball, it comes in the shape of the drill you see opposite, which involves standing with your back facing the target as you prepare to hit a ball located outside your left foot. I'm serious. Be in no doubt, from this position you will experience the sensation of the club approaching the ball on a shallow and severely inside path, and the right forearm will be forced to cross over the left as you release the club through the ball. Result? A raking draw.

Trust me when I tell you that this drill can cure even the most ingrained slice. The fact that there is now a release with the forearms will get the clubface squaring off and closing through the ball (hitherto qualities that have been lacking in your swing). Don't be afraid to give it a go – it's like a top-spin forehand in tennis. Enjoy the refreshing sensation of the clubface squaring through impact – slam it shut! Release the right hand and forearm and feel the shape of the shot in your swing. Sling the ball from right to left. The results will be worth the embarrassment. But don't be surprised if those practising nearby begin to shuffle a little further down the range…

• PUTTING •

How to make the 'money putts'

More short putts are missed because of a slight movement in the head or the body than anything else. As soon as you look up, or peek at the hole, you throw your stroke off line, and the ball with it. The trouble is, when you are within six or eight feet of the hole, and can see it out of the corner of your eye, it can be tempting to look up to follow the ball as you strike it. Tempting, but extremely dangerous. The key to holing these putts is to keep your head still so that you make solid contact and get the ball running on line. Double your effort on anything inside six feet – remind yourself to keep your head dead still as you make your stroke. To help you learn this discipline, press a coin into the green, place a ball on top of it, and spend five minutes on the practice green before you play knocking in putts from three or four feet, and look for that coin as you strike each one. Don't take your eyes off it until you hear the ball rattle in the cup.

• PUTTING •

How to get the ball truly lined up

I have long held the belief that the greatest putters in the world are those who really know how to get both themselves and the blade properly lined up on the greens. This is particularly critical from inside twenty feet or so, on the putts you really have a chance to make. If you study tour players in action you will see that they take exceptional care when marking and replacing their ball so that the script (or some personal logo) is aimed perfectly along their chosen line to the hole. This then provides them with a point of reference when it comes to making sure that the putter-face is perfectly aligned at address.

Hardly rocket science, but a simple and effective way of eliminating guesswork – and perfectly within the rules. All you have to do is get yourself a marker pen and draw a straight line on the ball. Then, once you have studied the line of a putt, carefully replace the ball so that the line on the ball reflects the line of the putt. Then it's a relatively simple matter of placing the putter-face squarely to the line on the ball, and there you have it: perfect alignment, which sets you up with total confidence.

• SAND PLAY •

Poor depth control? Keep your right foot grounded

If your bunker play on a normal to shorter length bunker shot is inconsistent in terms of the amount of sand you take, and your ability to control the distance you fly the ball is somewhat iffy, it may well be that you are getting onto your left side too quickly as you start down. When that happens you inevitably steepen the arc of your swing, which can lead to the club digging too deeply into the sand (thus eliminating the bounce effect). To get around that problem, focus on keeping your right foot planted throughout the whole of the downswing and in to the finish. The added width this will give you will shallow your swing and allow you to skim the clubhead through the sand on a much more playable angle – using that bounce to cut out a consistent divot of sand.

Bunker shots are really all about the hands, arms and upper body. There is no transfer of weight as such. Staying on your right side that little bit longer in the downswing allows you to get more aggressive with the hands and the arms through impact, and with practise you can really have some fun sliding the face through the sand beneath the ball and creating incredible backspin. (On a shot of 40 yards-plus, one of the toughest shots in golf, you have to use more lower body motion to create more clubhead speed.)

· THE SHORT GAME ·

Is your chipping on the button?

When it comes to chipping and pitching, adjusting the flight of your shots around the green is largely down to the way you position your body in relation to the ball at the set-up. If you want to hit it high, you need to get your body more behind the ball. To hit it low, you need to get your body more ahead of the ball. One of the easiest ways to think about this is to consider the position of your shirt buttons in relation

to the ball: To keep it low, ease your upper body (and those shirt buttons) ahead of the ball at the set-up (and don't forget to play the ball back in your stance). For a higher shot, move them back (and play the ball forward). This simple adjustment will bring about the change in the impact that you are looking for. Staying behind the ball adds loft for a higher, softer flight, getting your body ahead of it takes loft away.

• FAULT FIXING •

Emergency fixes for hooks and slices

Try this for an on-the-course cure next time you find yourself either beginning to hook or slice the ball. A simple grip and set-up adjustment can take care of the problem and get you back to the clubhouse for more permanent repairs later.

Slicing?

The moment you sense a slice coming on, check that as you set up to the ball your right arm is situated a little lower than the left. Then put the right hand in a 'stronger' position on the grip (i.e. turn it more under the shaft, to the right), and toe-in the clubface a fraction behind the ball (i.e. hood it slightly). Making your normal swing with these changes on board should help to drastically reduce your tendency to slice, and at least give you a playable shape for the remaining holes. Then you can get to work on a more permenant 'fix' with the help of your pro.

Hooking?

If you begin to get the hooks, you need to make the opposite adjustments. Set up to the ball with your upper body a little more open in relation to your target line, and get the right hand more on top of the grip, in what we term a 'weaker' position (i.e. turn it a little more to the left). These 'band-aid' fixes will help to compensate for the severe in-to-out path that has been causing you to spin the ball from right to left.

• RHYTHM & TEMPO •

To release tension, take last two fingers off the club...

The greater the pressure you face on the course, the greater the risk of you tightening your grip on the club. And there's the No.1 source of tension in golf: the grip. As soon as you tighten the fingers, you create a sort of muscular 'grid-lock' up through the arms and shoulders, which inevitably stifles your ability to create a *swing*. Here's a novel way to combat that problem next time you sense the pressure might be taking over. Slip the last two fingers of the left hand up off the end of the grip. Then put your right hand on. As soon as you do this you will feel and sense the clubhead. Instinctively you will swing more easily and freely, not trying to over-control the club. It is said Ben Hogan actually used to hit shots like this during tournaments whenever he felt tension. And that's the best endorsement anyone could give.

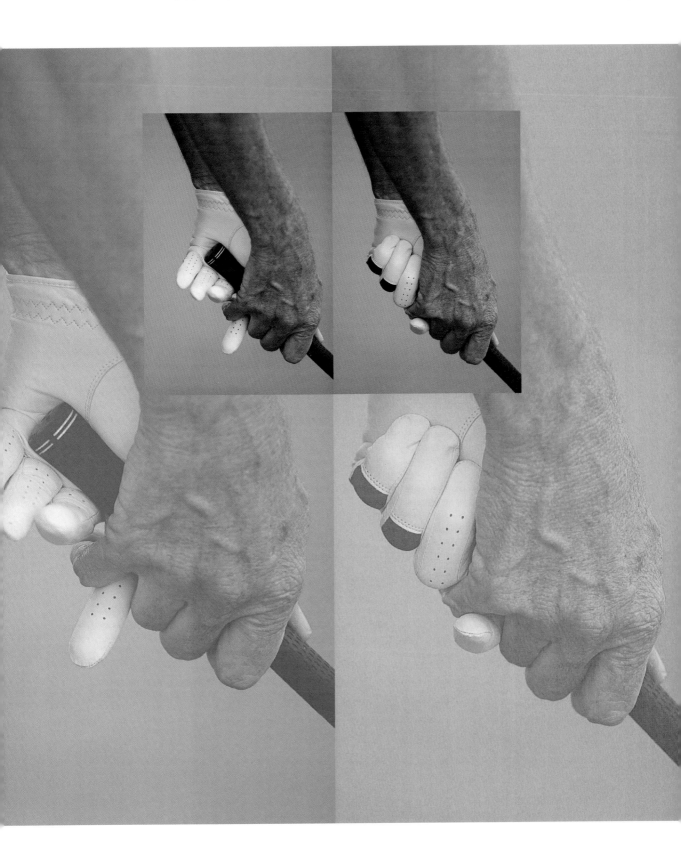

· PUTTING ·

Empty water bottle keeps your stroke on track

The art of synchronizing your body motion with the arms and hands is just as important with a putter in your hands as it is in the full swing. I'm not talking about creating a mechanical stroke to the point of it being 'wooden', but you do want to work on creating a solid framework that enables you to run the putter back and forth on a repeating path. The feel in your hands and arms has to enjoy that sort of back up. I see so many golfers who take the putter back too far outside or inside the line, with little consistency.

This exercise will help to correct that, and all you

need is an empty plastic water bottle. Stick it under your left arm, and make sure that as you swing back you maintain that pressure on your chest. It really makes the shoulders, arms and chest work *together*. And the more you maintain this relationship, the more reliable your stroke will be as you swing the putter back and through. Practice on the putting green, or on the carpet at home. Do it regularly, and in a very short space of time your putting will noticeably improve as you learn to control the stroke with the bigger, more dependable muscles in the upper body.

• JUST A THOUGHT •

Hang your arms... like strands of cooked spaghetti

One of the things that strikes me most when I watch a good player set-up to the ball is how 'soft' and comfortable the position looks. The hands seem to *caress* the grip, the arms are relaxed, and this sets the tone for the fluidity of the motion that follows. All this is in stark contrast to the tight and 'wooden' look that you often see in the anxious set-up of amateurs who grip the club so tightly that all feel for the swing is lost.

To get a sense of what I'm talking about, take a club, hold it at waist high and grip it as hard as you possibly can, so the muscles ripple in your arms and shoulders. Hold that clenched position for a couple of seconds, until your body almost begins to shudder under the pressure, and then relax. Totally exhale. Then do it again; tighten, and relax. As the tension drains from your body, your arms should feel soft, like strands of cooked spaghetti. And that's exactly the feeling I want you to have as you lower the clubhead to the ground and assume a normal position over the ball. Keeping those hands and arms relaxed at the set-up and through the initial stages of the backswing is a sure-fire key to enjoying a free and easy motion.

• PUTTING •

Pressure? Don't even think about it!

A sense of *flow* and a natural intuition with the putter are the intangible qualities good players seem to enjoy no matter what the pressure. This drill can help you to similarly free up your stroke to put a positive roll on those crucial three and four footers. It works like this. Set half a dozen balls around a hole, and then walk up and knock each one firmly into the heart without stopping to think about the line or your stroke. Make each putt a simple reflex motion – take one look at the hole and strike the ball firmly in. Just as simple as that. Practice this on the putting green before you go out to play a game: relax, one look and knock it in. This drill works because it takes away the thought that can so often lead to you getting too tight and tense over the ball. You don't want to be standing over a putt thinking about what it means to make it…or miss it. Free your mind, and you free your body.

· ACKNOWLEDGEMENTS ·

· PHOTOGRAPHS ·

All skills photography at the David Leadbetter Golf Academy,

Champions' Gate, Orlando, Florida courtesy of David Cannon/Allsport

All other photographs courtesy of Allsport Photographic.

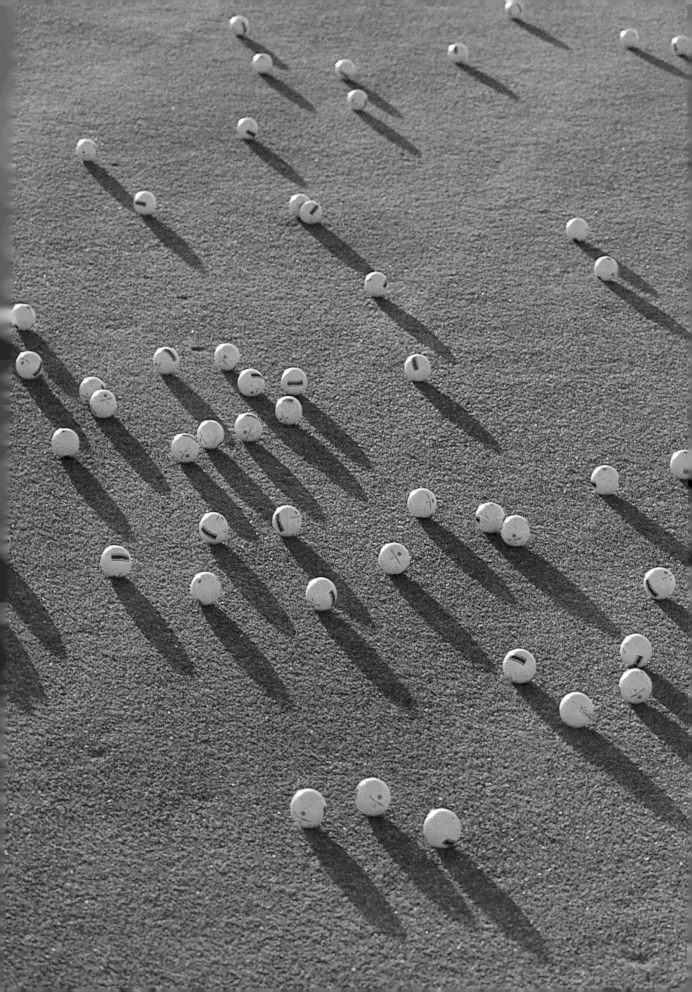